The I Ching
or
book of changes

The I Ching
or
book of changes

A Guide to Life's Turning Points

BRIAN BROWNE WALKER

PIATKUS

For David LaChapelle

First published in Great Britain in 1993
by Judy Piatkus (Publishers) Ltd of
5 Windmill Street, London W1P 1HF

**The moral right of the author
has been asserted**

*A catalogue record for this book is available
from the British Library*

ISBN 0-7499-1265-0

Design by Anne Scatto

Printed and bound in Great Britain by
Bookcraft Ltd, Midsomer Norton, Avon

The only true aristocracy is that of consciousness.

—*D. H. Lawrence*

INTRODUCTION TO THE *BOOK OF CHANGES*

This Is Just a Book

On its surface, the *I Ching* is merely a book. It is a very old book—one that has survived for thousands and thousands of years in many different forms—but it is just a book. It is also a very wise book—it is regarded as the foundation text of Chinese wisdom and philosophy and was instrumental to sages such as Confucius, whose education and teachings were formed by it—but it is just a book.

This Is More Than Just a Book

Beneath the surface, however, the *Book of Changes* is more than just a book. It is a living, breathing oracle, a patient and all-seeing teacher who can be relied upon for flawless advice at every turning point in our lives. Those who approach the *I Ching* sincerely, consult it regularly, and embody in their lives the lessons it teaches inevitably experience the greatest riches that life has to offer: prosperity, understanding, and peace of mind.

The *Book of Changes* speaks to us not in abstract platitudes but with direct advice about what to do *now*, in *this* situation, to bring about our own success and good fortune. It is for this reason that it is so dynamically alive today, thousands of years and thousands of miles from its place of origin.

What Does the *I Ching* Teach Us?

The *I Ching* takes a decidedly realistic view of the world. It doesn't mislead us into thinking that evil—in ourselves, in others, in the world at large—can be eliminated once and for all. It acknowledges that we all have in our characters both positive and negative elements, and it teaches us to be led by our superior qualities so that our thoughts and actions are free of inferior influences. It also teaches us how to respond to negative influences outside ourselves in order to avoid harm and maintain our well-being.

The qualities that the *Book of Changes* counsels us to embody in our lives are modesty, awareness, acceptance, adaptability, compassion, restraint, innocence, perseverance, tolerance, reticence, devotion to inner truth, patience, openness, detachment, conscientiousness, balance, and inner independence. The qualities that the *I Ching* urges us to let go of are fear, anger, desire, arrogance, aggressiveness, anxiety, harshness, cunning, goal orientation, and self-indulgence. At this point these are merely words. It is only when we begin to follow the guidance of the *I Ching* that we begin to have an inkling of their true meaning.

What Must We Bring to the *I Ching*?

The *Book of Changes* does not require that we be rich, smart, or beautiful in order to receive its teachings. It asks simply that we "meet it halfway." What is meant by this is that we approach the *I Ching* sincerely, putting aside our doubt and mistrust of the Unknown, with a willingness to reflect clearly upon our own character and to correct it when self-correction is advised. No matter how humble or desperate your current situation, if you will do this, you will inherit the good fortune that befalls devoted students of the *I Ching*.

About "the Sage"

In this text you will see references to "the Sage," "the Creative," "the Higher Power," and so on. The equivalent in your own mind may be "God," "Allah," "my higher self," "the universe," or some other term. Simply substitute the word or phrase that works comfortably for you.

Where to Begin

Read the instructions on the next page on how to consult the *I Ching*. You may ask for specific advice on a situation at hand, or you may consult the Sage just for general guidance. Many students of the *I Ching* throw a hexagram early in the morning as a way of giving a direction to the day. You should use it as you like. There are no rules governing how little or how often we ought to consult the oracle, only the reminder that we must approach it in sincerity if we wish to derive benefit. If you are prepared to do this, you are now standing on the threshold of a new life.

HOW TO CONSULT THE *I CHING*

1. Shake three coins in your closed hands and drop them.
2. Count heads as three and tails as two, and add the value of all three coins. Three heads equals nine, two heads and one tail equals eight, and so on.
3. If the number is odd, draw an unbroken line. If it is even, draw a line that is broken in the center. Write the numerical value of the line next to it.
4. Throw the coins again to get the second line of your hexagram. Draw this line *above*, not below, the first line.
5. Repeat this procedure until you have six stacked lines. Remember to proceed upward from the first line, not downward. Your hexagram might look like this:

SIXTH LINE	————————	9
FIFTH LINE	——— ———	8
FOURTH LINE	————————	7
THIRD LINE	————————	9
SECOND LINE	————————	7
FIRST LINE	——— ———	6

6. To find out which hexagram this is, consult the chart printed on pages 3 and 133 for convenient reference. The bottom three lines are the lower trigram, and the top three lines are the upper trigram. The number on the chart that lies at their intersection indicates which hexagram you have thrown. The example above is number 50.

7. Read the text for that hexagram up to the section that says "First line." Beyond that, read only the sections for those lines which "changed" in your hexagram. Changing lines are those with a value of 6 or 9. In the example above, lines 1, 3, and 6 are all changing lines.
8. Having read the hexagram's text and that for any changing lines, now convert the changing lines to their opposites. In the example above, the first line now becomes unbroken and the third and sixth lines become broken. Look up the new hexagram. In this example, it is number 54.
9. The text of the second hexagram is read to further illuminate the instruction of the first. Do not read the text for any lines, just read the opening paragraphs.

KEY FOR IDENTIFYING THE HEXAGRAMS

TRIGRAMS

UPPER ▶ / LOWER ▼	CH'IEN ☰ *Heaven*	CHÊN ☳ *Thunder*	K'AN ☵ *Water*	KÊN ☶ *Mountain*	K'UN ☷ *Earth*	SUN ☴ *Wind*	LI ☲ *Fire*	TUI ☱ *Lake*
CH'IEN ☰ *Heaven*	1	34	5	26	11	9	14	43
CHÊN ☳ *Thunder*	25	51	3	27	24	42	21	17
K'AN ☵ *Water*	6	40	29	4	7	59	64	47
KÊN ☶ *Mountain*	33	62	39	52	15	53	56	31
K'UN ☷ *Earth*	12	16	8	23	2	20	35	45
SUN ☴ *Wind*	44	32	48	18	46	57	50	28
LI ☲ *Fire*	13	55	63	22	36	37	30	49
TUI ☱ *Lake*	10	54	60	41	19	61	38	58

乾

HEAVEN

HEAVEN

1. CH'IEN/ THE CREATIVE

If you are alert to the Creative,
you will meet with good fortune now.

This hexagram signals a time when the fundamental creative power of the universe is available to you. An unrestricted outpouring of benevolent energy from the heavens makes possible profound progress for those who are conscientiously following proper principles.

Frantic activity is not in order. Your responsibility instead is to be open and receptive to the Higher Power, allowing it to guide your actions. By allowing inferior thoughts and habits to pass away, you make room for an expansion of your superior qualities, which leads inevitably to good fortune. In your conduct with others, embody tolerance, reticence, and gentleness. Strive to meet others halfway in every situation. To overextend yourself, or require that of another, is to create an undesirable imbalance.

Your attitude toward the Sage is most important. Alertness and receptiveness are paramount. To receive the powerful assistance of the Creative, remain humble, patient, accepting, and responsive. Careful attention to truth brings vast rewards at this time.

FIRST LINE Darkness still. Do not act prematurely. The light of the Creative has yet to emerge. Remain patient until the time is clearly ripe.

SECOND LINE The light begins to emerge. Resist the compulsions of the ego to influence others and gain recognition. Modesty furthers.

THIRD LINE Your inner power makes influence possible. There is danger in ambition and agenda-making. The truly beneficial influence is that which flows naturally from your attention to what is correct.

FOURTH LINE A place of transition. There is the possibility of progress in many directions. Let go of preconceived notions about your proper path. You succeed by allowing the Creative to guide you.

FIFTH LINE Your attention to proper principles has fostered an emergence of the Creative. Influence occurs without any conscious intervention on your part.

SIXTH LINE Arrogance in ambition or conduct brings danger, downfall, and isolation. Remain quietly joined to the will of the Sage. The abandonment of gentleness and humility leads to misfortune.

坤

EARTH

EARTH

2. K'UN/ THE RECEPTIVE

Bear with things as the earth bears with us:
by yielding, by accepting, by nourishing.

K'un the Receptive is the complement to Ch'ien the Creative: the dark which is illuminated by light, the earth which receives the blessings of heaven, the vessel into which nourishment flows. This is a time to follow rather than lead, to assist rather than initiate, to listen rather than talk. Redevote yourself to the cultivation of modesty, receptivity, and gentleness now, and let go of concerns about the conduct of others or the progress of your worldly ambitions.

The wisdom of cultivating receptivity cannot be overstated; receptivity is the rich earth without which the Creative cannot take root in our lives. This fundamental hexagram serves as a strong encouragement to you to concentrate on your capacities to nourish, to support, to accept, to work without desiring recognition, to follow the guidance of the Sage.

You can benefit greatly in a period like this from time spent in solitude; in quietness we have an opportunity to focus on the purification of our hearts and minds. It is a good time to ask oneself, "Am I sincerely pursuing the good for its own sake, or do I have a hidden agenda?" If so, detach from it and return to the path of independence and balance. Through humility and openness we become receptive to the assistance of the Higher Power.

FIRST LINE Cease resistance to the course of events. Avoid defensive or aggressive postures. The earlier one returns to quiet reliance on proper principles, the better.

SECOND LINE The solution to every situation is always available. By remaining open, innocent, and moderate you allow the Creative to aid you. Do less, not more.

THIRD LINE Vanity is an obstacle to the expression of our superior selves. Hold to inner truth without regard for popular opinion. Sincerity and humility open the way to a good fortune that cannot enter where arrogance flourishes.

FOURTH LINE Danger. The greatest possible reticence and reserve are in order. Resistance to events will result in a downfall.

FIFTH LINE True devotion to the good is unconcerned with what others may think or do. Concentrate not on having an influence but on doing the work of the Sage.

SIXTH LINE It is dangerous to engage in the thoughts and actions of the ego. Indulgence of negative emotions brings misfortune. Persevere in receptivity, reticence, and humility.

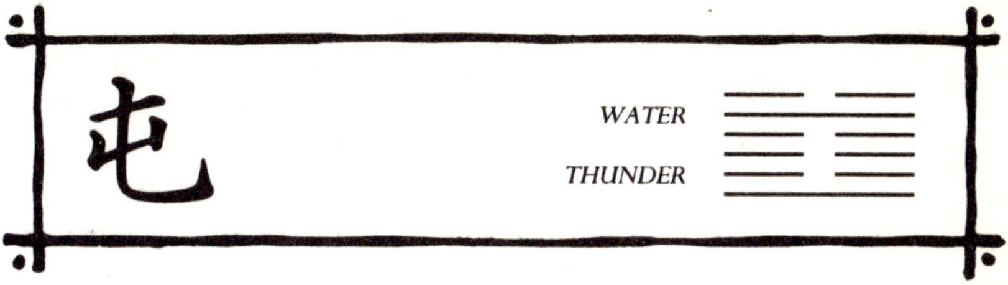

3. CHUN/ DIFFICULTY AT THE BEGINNING

If we persevere a great success is at hand.

The literal translation of "chun" is "a blade of grass pushing against an obstacle as it sprouts out of the earth." Receiving this hexagram is a sign that beyond the difficulties and pressures that surround you, a success lies waiting. In order to bring it fully into the light, you must be patient and persevere in nonaction.

No matter how fervently one desires to resolve a situation, to intervene impatiently now will only hinder the progress of good fortune. Accept and bear with the discomfort of chaos without attempting to push it away. Allowing it to clear of its own accord, in its own time, is the only way of insuring a subsequent blossoming of success.

Hold to proper principles. In your actions, seek and respect the counsel of the Sage. Allow those whose hearts are true to assist you wherever possible; be tolerant of all others. In this way the blessing that now lies hidden will come into the open.

FIRST LINE A difficulty at the beginning. Do not push aggressively, but do not give up. Accept the help of the Sage.

SECOND LINE A solution presents itself. While relief would be welcome, undesirable obligations may be created. Wait patiently for a solution that is correct in every particular.

THIRD LINE Do not act on your own. Seek the advice of the Sage and remain patient until the path is clearly shown.

FOURTH LINE An effort at union, made in humility and sincerity, and faithful to the principles of the Sage, will meet with good fortune.

FIFTH LINE Darkness distorts your light. Avoid attempting to force a completion. Go slowly, methodically, and with quiet balance.

SIXTH LINE Negative emotions tempt you to abandon your efforts. It is the greatest misfortune to do so. Hold fast to truth, and persevere.

蒙

MOUNTAIN

WATER

4. MÊNG/YOUTHFUL FOLLY

Even the foolish can attain wisdom
by modestly following the Sage.

Folly is a characteristic of youth: those who have had little experience generally exhibit little wisdom. This is true of us in a spiritual way as well; in comparison to the Sage we are "babes in the woods." The hexagram Mêng counsels us to utilize the *I Ching* as a lantern so that we may survive our youthful folly and travel safely through the woods of life.

There is no shame in seeking guidance in life. A child is eager to be shown the way by his parents and teachers, and we are wise to recognize that in spiritual terms we are akin to children. Our success will come quicker if we find and follow a wise teacher. The Sage is available to serve in this way for those who approach the *I Ching* with a sincere desire to learn and grow.

To study the *I Ching* is to gain the perspective of the Deity, to learn the cosmic lesson inherent in every situation that faces us. If we truly look for and strive to comprehend these larger lessons, we gain mastery over fear, doubt, and anxiety. We can learn from study of the *I Ching* to live in a state of understanding, contentment, and acceptance, but several things are required of us.

The first is that we suspend our mistrust of the Unknown and allow the Sage to lead us. It is tempting to think that the *I Ching* might be just a book, merely words on paper, but there is more to it than this. To accept this is to recognize the Sage and become receptive to his assistance.

The second thing required of us is that we quiet the demands of our egos for comprehensive answers to our questions about life. The *I Ching* teaches us not how to get from A to Z but how to get from A to B, then from B to C, then from C to D. The Sage travels step by step, dealing always with what is immediately at hand and bringing complete focus and concentration to the moment. By doing the same we fall into step with, and receive the help of, the Creative power of the universe.

Lastly, we are required to unstructure our attitude. By abandoning strategies about people and situations, we let the past and future go and meet the present with an open mind. To be unstructured and open is to allow the Sage to guide us safely and joyfully through life.

The image of Mêng is that of a stream beginning to flow down a mountainside, filling each ravine and hollow place as it goes. If we persevere in following the Sage, seeking the counsel of the *I Ching*, and filling in the gaps in our character as they are revealed, we will be led to lasting success in life.

FIRST LINE Those who toy with life never attain mastery. Self-discipline and courageous contemplation are necessary steps to understanding. However, do not become over-zealous and drill yourself into the ground.

SECOND LINE You are wise to bear with inferior elements patiently and kindly. The best way to have an influence now is to cultivate inner strength and outer calm.

THIRD LINE A servile attitude toward the Sage is of no use. The door opens not when we are browbeaten into accepting truth but when we begin to see its value and seek it on our own.

FOURTH LINE Those who entangle themselves in the fears and fantasies of the ego lose the aid of the Sage. A return to detachment and humility prevents misfortune now.

FIFTH LINE Children make the best students. Seek truth in an open and unstructured manner and the secrets of the universe will be revealed.

SIXTH LINE A determined fool has to be punished, but should not be executed. If you are the fool, accept the lesson and go on in correctness. If the fool is another, let him go and leave the punishment to the Sage.

需

5. HSÜ / WAITING (NOURISHMENT)

To wait with a proper attitude
invites the assistance of the Higher Power.

There is a situation at hand that cannot be corrected by force or external effort. The Creative will provide the solution to one who waits with a correct attitude. This is a time for patience and careful attention to inner truth.

Do not give in to doubt and agitation now. You are not meant to wait in a state of desperate longing but in one of patient inner strength. Without certainty in the power of truth, success is impossible. Attempts to force a change, rather than allowing it to mature naturally, will only cause misfortune.

You would be wise to strengthen and reaffirm your reliance on the Creative. When you indulge in fear and doubt, you flood the arena where the Higher Power is attempting to work. Your principal responsibility in life is to keep this arena—your own consciousness—free of negative influences.

By accepting things as they are and not making fruitless comparisons to the situations of others or some imagined ideal, one engages the power of the Creative. If one then remains balanced, modest, and independent, good fortune will come to hand.

FIRST LINE A challenge lies ahead. Ready yourself by deepening the stillness within. Anxious anticipation only weakens your abilities.

SECOND LINE Danger draws closer. Do not be pulled off balance or act rashly. Cultivate humility, correctness, and stillness.

THIRD LINE There is a danger of being swayed from a correct attitude. To allow this invites misfortune. Return to the strength of proper principles.

FOURTH LINE Great danger. Hardness toward others or the Sage spills one's own blood. Return to humility.

FIFTH LINE A moment of peace in the midst of difficulty. Make use of occasions for rest while preparing within for further challenges.

SIXTH LINE A solution appears that at first glance seems strange. Waiting with an open mind and a quiet heart allows you to accept truth in whatever form it arrives.

訟

HEAVEN

WATER

6. SUNG/ CONFLICT

The proper response to conflict, whether it lies within or without us, is disengagement.

Whenever we allow ourselves to be drawn off balance, away from the strength of quiet integrity, we are in conflict. It matters not whether the confrontation is between competing values in one's own mind or with another person: it is the inner departure from clarity and equanimity that leaves us with feelings of despair and vulnerability. The only remedy is to disengage from the problem and return to quiet contemplation of what is correct.

Conflict provokes strong feelings of doubt, fear, anxiety, and impatience to resolve the situation. If you act under the influence of these inferior emotions, you will severely complicate the misfortune. By following the prescription of the Sage and returning to a position of neutrality, acceptance, and detachment, you are able to meet opposing forces halfway: not recoiling in anger and condemnation, not pressing forward for some unnatural change in things, but waiting calmly in the center until the Higher Power provides the correct solution.

The *I Ching* teaches us that all conflict is, in the end, inner conflict. When you see it beginning, you are obliged not to pursue it, for this only compounds your own misfortune. If you cannot regain your equanimity on your own, then seek the assistance of a just and impartial person in resolving the difficulty. The only way to live free of conflict is to hold steadfastly to proper principles in all things. Through balance, patience, and devotion to inner truth we rise above every challenge.

FIRST LINE The best time to resolve a conflict is at the beginning. Disengage your ego, and you meet with good fortune.

SECOND LINE The excesses of the ego can lead us into slaughter. The superior person maintains his humility and his calm and allows the Sage to work things out.

THIRD LINE Do not fight with others for center stage. That which is truly valuable is gained through quiet perseverance, modesty, and a sincere devotion to the Sage.

FOURTH LINE All true progress is made on a path of correctness. If your desire to achieve an end is drawing you off this path, turn back. In returning to conscientiousness you meet with success.

FIFTH LINE One is wise to turn the conflict over to the jurisdiction of the Sage or a just arbiter. Good fortune obtains.

SIXTH LINE You may achieve a temporary gain by worrying the matter to its bitter end, but the long-term price you pay for this will be great. It is wiser to simply let it go.

師

EARTH

WATER

7. SHIH/THE ARMY

In times of war it is desirable
to be led by a cautious and humane general.

The hexagram Shih is a guide to proper conduct in the face of adversity. It is inevitable that we sometimes face trials and challenges in life. How we prepare ourselves, by whom we are led, and how we conduct ourselves during these "wars" determines whether we are victorious or not. The *I Ching* counsels us to follow the example of a first-rate army.

A truly powerful army always consists of a number of devoted soldiers who discipline themselves under the leadership of a superior general. If he has achieved his position through force, the general will not last for long and he will lose the support of his army when he needs it most. If on the other hand he has become a leader through superior conduct and even-handed treatment of his fellow soldiers, then his power is well consolidated and it endures.

So it is with us. Only by conducting ourselves humanely and with persevering balance can we have a genuine influence in trying times. There is always the temptation to be led into battle by our egos, but we are guaranteed a humiliating defeat if we turn our inferiors loose in this way. A superior person achieves victory in the same fashion as a superior army: by putting his inferior emotions under the guidance of his superior emotions, and by proceeding cautiously, modestly, and with the continual goal of achieving peace and detachment.

You are advised to prepare for a trial now. Your chances of success will be determined by how you conduct yourself within and without.

If you remain alert, modest, just, and independent, all will go well. If you are gentle and humane, you will have the allegiance of those around you. Advance cautiously when the time is right, and when it is not, do not allow your ego to stand in the way of retreat and disengagement.

Remember that the ultimate victory in any battle comes when we regain our inner independence, our neutrality, and our equanimity. These can only be won by placing our inferiors under the leadership of our superiors. Do this now, and success will be yours.

FIRST LINE Be certain that your cause is truly just. If so, next be certain that your conduct is modest, generous, and balanced. Otherwise your ego leads you into disaster.

SECOND LINE It is the task of the superior self to reassure the inferior self. Follow the Sage at every step, reminding yourself regularly of the wisdom of this path.

THIRD LINE Inferior influences have taken control of the situation. Unless the ego is disciplined, there is defeat and humiliation in store. Patience and disengagement are called for now.

FOURTH LINE When inferiors are at work in us or in others, it is wise to disengage and retreat. No victory can be won until detachment and equanimity are restored.

FIFTH LINE Evil has come back into the open. To correct it, withdraw into stillness and contemplate proper principles. Lashing out will only compound the misfortune.

SIXTH LINE If victory is sought immodestly, there will be humiliation. Lasting progress is won slowly and steadily through the exercise of proper principles.

比

WATER

EARTH

8. PI/HOLDING TOGETHER (UNION)

Seek union with others and with the Sage.

"Holding together" denotes a time for creating union with others in order to complement and assist one another, just as the rain complements and assists the earth, which is an image often associated with this hexagram. In order for your unions to bear the greatest possible fruit, certain requirements must be met.

The first requirement for holding together with others is that we hold together with our own inner truth. This means that we adhere to proper principles as a matter of habit, striving always to remain innocent, balanced, and correct. In short, marry the Sage first and faithfully, and good fortune will come to all subsequent marriages.

The second requirement for holding together with others is that we steadfastly resist the clamoring of the emotional inferiors within. Every union meets with challenges, and if we are not resolute against the effects of fear, doubt, despair, and anger, no lasting success will be possible in any relationship. This is a good time to ask yourself if you are displaying the steadfast correctness and strength of character that are at the heart of all great unions.

Finally, it is the responsibility of one who would unite to see that it is possible for others to enjoy union as well. The desire for community is deeply felt by all humans, and it is the shared responsibility of all those on the higher path to make some sort of "family" available to those in need. In doing this, we pay homage to the Sage.

FIRST LINE A genuine commitment to truth is the fundamental building block of all relationships. Where this is not present there can be no union.

SECOND LINE Do not throw yourself away by worshipping inferiors. Maintaining proper principles maintains one's dignity.

THIRD LINE There is a danger of uniting with the wrong elements. Correct your attitude and review your alliances. Without independence and integrity you meet with misfortune.

FOURTH LINE Remain constant in the use of proper principles and success will surround you.

FIFTH LINE Proper relationships flow from proper principles. Do not cling to others, but to your own neutrality, humility, and steady devotion to truth. Allow others to come and go as they must.

SIXTH LINE Proceed firmly but with caution. Only by paying careful attention to each step does one arrive unharmed. This means acting in every particular as if you were the Sage himself.

小畜

WIND

HEAVEN

9. HSIAO CH'U/ THE TAMING POWER OF THE SMALL

You are temporarily restrained.
It is a time for taking small steps.

This hexagram signifies a time when darkness has temporarily enveloped the light. The Creative power is present in the background, however, and will come forward in time. Your responsibility in this moment is to accept restraints quietly and remain content with taking small steps.

The obstacles to success can only be removed now by gentle measures. Inside yourself, be focused and determined. On the outside, nonaction, adaptability, neutrality, and tolerance are the order of the day. Ambitious behavior is to be avoided; think of planting seeds rather than harvesting fruit.

Do not forget that the inferior elements within yourself, others, and the time itself may only be restrained now—not fully removed. Do not be tempted into any engagement which will serve to unbalance you. Instead, hold quietly to the center and take small steps until the Higher Power has tamed the obstacles in your way.

FIRST LINE It is imprudent to attempt to force a change. Neither should you lapse into the despair that is caused by impatience. Remain steadfastly humble and accepting.

SECOND LINE You may see from your intuition or the experience of others that the way is not open. If so, remain in the quiet company of the Sage and renew your devotion to truth.

THIRD LINE To rush things is to invite misfortune. Do not collapse into anxiety, doubt, or the strategies of the ego. Letting go brings inner freedom.

FOURTH LINE Do not resort to incorrect means or disaster results. Treat others with the gentleness and dignity of the Sage. Maintain a detached stance.

FIFTH LINE One's greatest asset is an abiding loyalty to proper principles. Your good fortune is doubled if you share it with others.

SIXTH LINE Success is imminent. However, only by moving forward cautiously and conscientiously can you come into possession of it. There is danger in rushing.

履

HEAVEN

LAKE

10. LÜ / TREADING (CONDUCT)

Lasting progress is won
through quiet self-discipline.

This hexagram outlines the foundation of proper conduct within ourselves, with those with whom we may have conflicts, and within the larger society. It serves to remind us that no genuine gains can be made unless we are rooted firmly in the principles of the Sage.

An image often associated with this hexagram is that of treading on the tail of a tiger. The "tiger" may be some strong or malevolent force in your own personality, or it may be a particularly volatile individual or situation with which you have to deal. In either case the advice of the *I Ching* is the same: one avoids the bite of a tiger by treading carefully. To tread carefully means that we remain steadfastly innocent and conscientious in our thoughts and actions.

It is inevitable that people will display varying levels of spiritual understanding. It is not our duty to condemn or correct others, but simply to go on developing ourselves. Do not imagine that you can hasten your progress through aggressive actions now. Power that is sought and wielded pridefully has a way of evaporating when you need it most, thus exacerbating your difficulties. The only lasting influence is that which arises naturally from a course of steady self-development.

In the end, it is our inner worth that determines the outer conditions of our lives. Those who resolve to persevere in humility, sincerity, and gentleness can tread anywhere—even on the tail of a tiger—and meet with success.

FIRST LINE Ambition and restlessness lead to misfortune. A return to simplicity and humility makes progress possible now.

SECOND LINE The wise student travels his path with acceptance and contentment, remaining free of entanglements and conflicts. In this way there is happiness.

THIRD LINE Do not undertake something which exceeds your strength out of an impulse of the ego. Good fortune is met by those who remain modest and allow the Sage to make whatever corrections are necessary.

FOURTH LINE Move ahead cautiously and conscientiously. Your goal is met if you remain devoted to expressing higher things.

FIFTH LINE Others must be allowed to find their own way. Be friendly, but cling to correctness, humility, and detachment from events. Inner independence leads to good fortune.

SIXTH LINE Acceptance and inner balance move mountains that striving cannot. The fruit of good fortune springs from the seed of good conduct.

泰

EARTH

HEAVEN

11. T'AI/ PEACE

Heaven exists on earth for those who maintain correct thoughts and actions.

This hexagram signifies a time similar to spring: there is a strong flow of energy, and harmony and prosperity are the reward of those who correctly balance their higher and lower natures. It is by remaining aware of our inferior self while insuring that the superior self governs our conduct that we arrive in a state of peace.

See yourself as a young tree now. The ground around you is fertile; sun and water and wind are plentiful. By maintaining your focus on moving upward toward light, clarity, and purity you can reach great heights. If you become entangled in inferior things, you will not enjoy the full benefit of this gracious hour. Stay balanced, innocent, and correct, and good fortune is assured.

FIRST LINE A good time to act, if one's inner attitude is open and humble.

SECOND LINE Do not become dependent on a peaceful state of affairs. Bear with difficult people and situations generously. Act to further the work of the Sage in the world around you.

THIRD LINE Peace and harmony do not go on indefinitely. Ebb and flow are inherent in the nature of life. When difficulties arise, accept this and hold firmly to what is correct.

Good fortune returns to those who remain calm and detached.

FOURTH LINE Do not seek to impress or influence others. Meet them instead with sincerity, simplicity, and openness. In this way success is assured.

FIFTH LINE Remain patient until the Creative does its work. Modesty will bring greater rewards than the aggressive maneuverings of the ego.

SIXTH LINE A waning is at hand. Avoid resisting this or concocting strategies to escape it. We are aided when we submit to the wisdom of the Higher Power.

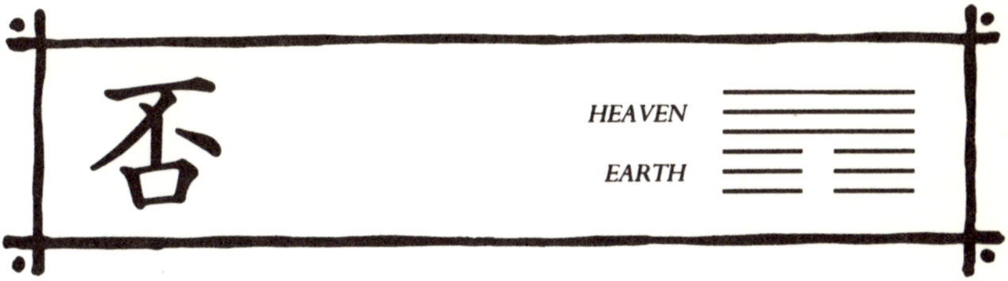

12. P'I/ STANDSTILL (STAGNATION)

In times of stagnation, attend to your attitude.

It is an unavoidable fact of life that inferior influences sometimes prevail: improperly motivated people ascend to power, there is injustice and conflict and poverty, and spiritual life in general descends into darkness and decay. While these difficult times are inevitable—and the arrival of this hexagram indicates that this is such a time—this does not mean that we have to stagnate personally as well. By turning inward and realigning ourselves with proper principles, we initiate the return to light, truth, and progress.

The image of P'i is of heaven moving away from the earth. When this happens, the inferior qualities in ourselves and in others come to the surface and seek expression. It is unlikely now that you can affect what others do and say or that your activities will bear much fruit. While it is natural to feel anxious and disappointed about this state of affairs, it is essential to disengage from these inferior emotions now. To indulge in them is to abandon your superior self and plunge into a state of disintegration.

What is wise now is to accept that external progress is unlikely. Turn your attention inward and examine your own thoughts and attitudes for inferior influences and departures from the principles of the Sage. By withdrawing into solitude and refining your higher nature, you continue to grow while all else around you stagnates.

FIRST LINE There is no opportunity to have an influence now.

Quiet your demanding ego and disengage from the situation while it is still easy. The Creative will aid you only if you step back into neutrality and equanimity.

SECOND LINE Be patient with inferior elements in yourself and others. By persevering in humility, gentleness, and openness, you rescue yourself and others as well.

THIRD LINE Those who have been incorrect will in time feel shame. Make no judgments; simply stay on the path of what is right. Then others can you join you and there will be good fortune.

FOURTH LINE Only when you allow yourself to be led by the Sage can you lead others. Concentrate on being modest and correct, and the situation will improve.

FIFTH LINE A change is at hand, but good fortune can only be maintained by those who are conscientious and correct in good times as well as bad. Do not allow your ego to take control.

SIXTH LINE The standstill can be ended by the efforts of a superior person. Allow the Sage to guide you in this, and good fortune will be met.

同人

HEAVEN

FIRE

13. T'UNG JÊN/ FELLOWSHIP WITH OTHERS

In fellowship with others,
embody the principles of the Sage.

This hexagram addresses the proper basis for relationships with others. It generally comes as a sign that some kind of self-correction is in order in this arena.

Proper relationships, whether in love, work, family, or friendship, must be founded on and conducted under proper principles in order to succeed. Our model for how to behave with others is the Sage: in relating we are obliged to practice kindness, humility, correctness, equanimity, and openness. Wherever we depart from these we lose the aid of the Higher Power and risk an encounter with misfortune.

The fundamental rule of the *I Ching* for the conduct of relationships is that they take place in the open. This means that every facet of a relationship should be seen as fair and correct by *everyone* concerned, not just yourself. It also means that it is improper to enter into or continue in relationships with unspoken reservations or hidden intentions.

Exceptional things can be accomplished by those who come together correctly in fellowship now under the guidance of an enlightened leader or leaders. Seek that role by patterning yourself after the Sage. Meet others halfway in a spirit of sincerity and receptivity. Give trust where it is due; where it is not, do not resort to harshness—reserve and reticence are adequate measures. Avoid the formation of factions and cliques, and correct your errors in relationships as soon as you become aware of them. In this way you can accomplish magnificent deeds now.

FIRST LINE Hidden intentions or agendas of the ego prevent proper fellowship. Meet in the open without ambitions, and cling to what is correct.

SECOND LINE Do not form factions, either by excluding others or by failing to correct yourself in some way. Misfortune results when unity and truth are ignored.

THIRD LINE Mistrust and secrets only lead to more mistrust and secrets. No good comes of this. Turn matters over to the Sage and follow his guidance.

FOURTH LINE Do not continue to fight and quarrel. It is better to disengage and separate. Perseverance in proper principles brings success in spite of all other influences.

FIFTH LINE An outward separation will come to an end in time. What is important now is to remain united in your heart with another. The path leads back to happiness.

SIXTH LINE Reservations about the wisdom of the way of the Sage prevent true fellowship. When you eliminate these in yourself, many doors are opened.

大有

FIRE

HEAVEN

14. TA YU/ POSSESSION IN GREAT MEASURE

Those who are steadfastly balanced, humble, and in harmony with the Sage inherit everything under the sun.

This is a time of great power and clarity for you. By conscientiously following the path of proper principles, you have come into partnership with the Higher Power and enjoy the influence of the Creative everywhere in your life. If you remain modest and balanced now, you will come into possession of prosperity and success.

The *I Ching* indicates here that you increased your personal power by purifying your thoughts, actions, and attitudes. When you have done this long enough so that service of the true and good becomes your only goal in life, you come into complete harmony with the universe. As a result, you begin to have a far-reaching influence, shining on others as the sun shines on everything under the heavens. Because your power is so great, it is especially important to maintain correct attitudes and behavior now.

Having attained a high position, you are wise to remain modest and generous toward others. Remember that it is the Higher Power who gives you your strength. Do not make the mistake of becoming proud, disdainful of others, or convinced of your ability to control events. By leaving the Sage in charge, withdrawing from all inferior influences, and promoting the good wherever possible, you remain gracefully balanced and in harmony with the universe. Your peace of mind becomes permanent, and in this way you come into possession of success and prosperity.

FIRST LINE In the early days your peace of mind will be challenged. By maintaining humility, detachment, and alertness to the approach of evil, you insure that your greatest possession endures.

SECOND LINE The most valuable possessions are equanimity, modesty, and inner independence. With these you can travel anywhere and meet with good fortune.

THIRD LINE This is a time when the superior person lets go of what is incorrect in himself and gives to others what is good in himself. Only a petty person is selfish with his possessions.

FOURTH LINE Do not indulge in looking at those around you and trying to match them tit for tat. You elevate yourself by disengaging and holding firmly to what is quiet and correct and good.

FIFTH LINE Do not chase others to try and influence them. Your knowledge of truth should be shared modestly and sincerely with those who are naturally drawn to it.

SIXTH LINE By conscientiously honoring the Sage you remain modest and good. The fullest blessings of the universe fall on those who are devoted in this way.

謙

EARTH

MOUNTAIN

15. CH'IEN/ MODESTY

The Creative acts to empty what is full
and to offer abundance to what is modest.

This hexagram suggests that a deepening of one's modesty now is a sure means of improving the situation. There is no power so great as modesty for compelling the assistance of the Sage—nor one so hindering as immodesty. Those in high places who retain their modesty are loved by all and continually prosper; those below who cultivate modesty inevitably rise on the strength of their merits, without making enemies along the way.

But what does modesty mean? Certainly it entails a refusal to boast or act imperiously with others, even in small ways. But beyond this steadfast humility it also means that our effort to discern what is right and then do it is constant; we do not work against ourselves, and we do not indulge in doubts about the wisdom of correct conduct. This unwavering commitment to what is correct might be called "the modesty before the Sage."

So there is in modesty a component of nonaction—that is, not indulging in arrogant, ego-centered behavior—as well as a component of active effort: looking for opportunities to correct ourselves, to assist justice where there is injustice, to feed where there is hunger, to give solace where there is pain.

Finally and most plainly, modesty means holding to innocence, sincerity, and openness in every situation. To do this is to empty yourself and make room for the blessings of the Creative to take root.

FIRST LINE Be modest about your modesty and do not look for recognition or reward. Good fortune accrues to one who remains unassuming and correct.

SECOND LINE The deeper one's modesty, the greater one's good fortune. Use good times to carefully reexamine your attitude, and your reward is multiplied.

THIRD LINE Do not pause in your progress to bask in admiration or anticipate results. Clinging to modesty affords you a greater success.

FOURTH LINE Do not make a show of modesty. Sincerity entails doing what is needed, without regard for public opinion, then quietly stepping back.

FIFTH LINE A time for moving forward with strength. This does not mean that we can deviate from correct behavior. To do so undermines the action.

SIXTH LINE Modesty does not allow for anger, self-righteousness, pride, or self-pity. The superior person stands guard against his own inferior elements.

豫

THUNDER

EARTH

16. YÜ/ ENTHUSIASM

Proper enthusiasm opens every door.

The *I Ching* teaches that there are two kinds of enthusiasm: one that leads to misfortune, and one that leads to success. This hexagram comes as a sign that you can proceed with confidence now if your enthusiasm is properly founded.

Improper enthusiasm is fueled by the desires of the ego. People often desire recognition, wealth, power, or freedom from difficulty. Such desires can become so great that we will do anything to achieve them. Our energy rises as we wildly pursue our goal, but this unruly and egotistical enthusiasm inevitably leads us into incorrect and imbalanced behavior and into misfortune.

Proper enthusiasm, on the other hand, is fueled by a devotion to attaining and expressing inner balance and inner truth. When your aim is not to influence others or to satisfy your ego but to follow the guidance of the Higher Power in all that you do, you acquire another kind of energy: a balanced and bottomless eagerness for living in step with what is right and good. In this there is true power and true grace.

This hexagram reminds you that striving out of your ego now will only push you further away from your goals. Seek instead to follow proper principles: keep to what is innocent, correct, and kind, and the Creative will come to your aid. The path of truth is always the path of least resistance.

FIRST LINE Arrogance leads to a fall. Unite with the Higher Power and remain modest and innocent.

SECOND LINE Recognize the beginnings of improper action. The superior person corrects herself while it is still easy to do so.

THIRD LINE Don't rely on others to direct your conduct. Be determined in holding to the good at every turn.

FOURTH LINE Devotion to what is right attracts the aid and fellowship of others. The greatest success comes to the one who is most sincere.

FIFTH LINE Your ego prevents the desired movement. Take time now to correct your inner attitude.

SIXTH LINE Inferior notions lead you toward misfortune. Self-correction can still make possible a success.

隨

LAKE
THUNDER

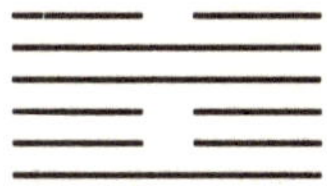

17. SUI/ FOLLOWING

Do not argue with what is;
simply follow the progress of truth.

Wisdom teaches us that in order to obtain a following—the aid and agreement of others—we must first ourselves practice following. This is done by steadfastly observing what is correct and putting it into practice; in other words, we follow the Sage. This hexagram comes to remind you to make it possible for others to be loyal and helpful to you by redevoting yourself to following inner truth.

It is essential now to quietly accept the way that things are. This does not necessarily mean that you endorse or celebrate current circumstances, just that you do not resist them. Acceptance is the most fundamental principle in the philosophy of the *I Ching*. To resist events is similar to resisting the turning of the earth—you only exhaust yourself in vain.

To resolve a difficult situation, follow the good within yourself. Whatever correction is necessary is made possible in this way. The use of force or cunning will only breed resentment and misfortune. Peace blooms quickest where proper principles are given expression.

Leading others is a delicate art, and our model in this is always the Sage. Proceed gently, with balance, staying unattached to results and free of egotistical pretensions. Lead the people by following the Sage, and a good result will always be had.

FIRST LINE Remain responsive to the views of those you would influence. Listen attentively for truth, even from unlikely sources, and discuss without quarreling.

SECOND LINE Do not cling to what is inferior, either in yourself or others. If a person or thought or practice is not in harmony with the principles of the Sage, quietly let go.

THIRD LINE Sometimes following the good requires that we forego a pleasure of the ego. When some part of your self-image would separate you from truth, let it fall away.

FOURTH LINE Following creates success. If others flatter you, maintain your innocence and modesty. Attend to what is good and allow others to come and go as they please.

FIFTH LINE Success comes from following what is good and true and innocent in every moment—especially those moments when you are inclined to do otherwise.

SIXTH LINE What is needed in the moment comes out of one's allegiance to the Sage. If this is constant and steadfast, then there is no lack.

蠱

MOUNTAIN

WIND

18. KU/ WORK ON WHAT HAS BEEN SPOILED (DECAY)

A challenge to improvement:
that which has been spoiled through neglect
can be rejuvenated through effort.

Receiving this hexagram is a sign that there is a defect in the attitude of oneself, another, or one's society that should be corrected. Your task now is to bring conscientious thought and action to an area where stagnation has set in. Perhaps you engage in continual doubt about the wisdom of behaving according to proper principles. Perhaps you indulge in greed, or vengeful thinking, or a harsh manner. In any case, the time has come to root out the decay.

The *I Ching* counsels us to work energetically at this task, but only after proper deliberation. We are advised to spend three full days in understanding the defect; another day in resolving sincerely to remove it; and then three more days watching carefully to insure that it does not return. This steady application of attention to the matter is the wind that carries away stagnation and brings new life in its place.

It is likely that the problem is an old one, and equally likely that no solution will be immediately evident. We are cautioned not to abandon the cause: only perseverance will reveal the great reward that is concealed within the problem.

Whether the fault lies in yourself, another, or your community, the requirement is the same. Watch closely while remaining quiet, innocent, and sincere. After you have clearly identified the problem, act unswervingly to eliminate it without abandoning gentleness and inner balance in the process. When this course is completed, good fortune will be met.

FIRST LINE The decay stems from adherence to a family tradition. Only by releasing the spoiled way of acting or thinking can you make room for superior influences. Let go freely.

SECOND LINE An underlying fear keeps you from seeing the truth. Be gentle but persistent with yourself in locating and releasing it.

THIRD LINE To proceed too vigorously in righting mistakes is to invite discord. However, no serious harm results as long as the imbalance is not excessive. More effort is better than less at this time.

FOURTH LINE Tolerating what is wrong leads to ruin. Decay must be met with clarity and firmness if we are to progress.

FIFTH LINE An obligation to aid or accept a continuing wrong may be felt. No such obligation exists. Your duty is always to uphold proper principles; to choose otherwise is to invite misfortune.

SIXTH LINE A withdrawal from the affairs of the world is appropriate if you use this time not to condemn, but to further your own development. By improving yourself you improve the world.

臨

EARTH

LAKE

19. LIN/ APPROACH

Good approaches the superior person.

The hexagram Lin signals the approach of powerful beneficial influences. Just as the winter solstice heralds the return of spring, the appearance of this hexagram marks a similar movement toward light and growth. Progress and success are assured now to those who persevere on the path of truth.

To maximize the opportunity implicit in this moment, it is important to cultivate a proper attitude. It is easy, during good times, to relax our inner discipline and fall back into incorrect thoughts and actions. Allowing one's ego to take over in a moment of success is a sure means of ending the progress that has begun. The growth that is at hand was made possible by conscientious behavior, and continuing carefully along that path is our only means of coming into full possession of it.

A steadfast modesty and acceptance, whether external conditions are good or bad, is the mark of the superior person. In yourself, maintain balance, equanimity, and humility in times of accomplishment. With others, remain patient, tolerant, and gentle. Clinging to these principles assures you of a time of joy and prosperity.

FIRST LINE Meet the beginning of good times with a correct attitude. Do not depart from equanimity into ambition and desire.

SECOND LINE Alliance with the Sage insures progress in good times and bad. Accept external conditions and maintain inner discipline.

THIRD LINE There is danger of relapsing into impurity and irresponsibility. An influential person must take care to uphold proper principles, or misfortune occurs.

FOURTH LINE Remaining open to the abilities of others, whatever their position, insures a greater success.

FIFTH LINE Help from others and from the Sage is attracted by modesty and correctness. One who acts alone out of his ego cannot achieve lasting success.

SIXTH LINE A greathearted person achieves great progress. Guide others by allowing the Sage to guide you.

觀

WIND

EARTH

20. KUAN/ CONTEMPLATION

By concentrating on the higher laws
you acquire the power that underlies them.

In Chinese the word "kuan" can mean either "contemplation" or "setting an example," depending upon how it is pronounced. This hexagram incorporates both meanings, for what it teaches us is to set an example for others through our own contemplation of proper principles.

A fundamental fact of consciousness is that we take on the attributes and energy of that upon which we focus our attention. In studying and meditating on the *I Ching*, we are concentrating on the underlying principles that govern the universe. Through contemplation of the wisdom of such principles as independence, detachment, modesty, acceptance, and tolerance, we begin to embody them in our own lives. Their power informs our actions and practices, and we begin to have great influence as a result.

This hexagram comes to indicate that you need to make a self-correction and return to contemplation of proper principles. By sacrificing the harsh judgments of your ego and asking the Sage for guidance, you free yourself from hindering influences and increase your merit—and thereby your ability to have an influence.

It is in the quiet contemplation of what is correct that we become detached from anxious emotions about the situations that face us. This detachment gives us the balance and calm to choose solutions which are in accordance with the higher laws. In so doing we gain the aid of the Creative in everything we do, and others are drawn to this strength. Truly, we gain the ability to lead through contemplation of the principles of our own leader, the Sage.

FIRST LINE Others may not yet recognize the correctness of following truth. The superior person leads them to this by deepening her own contemplation.

SECOND LINE Do not take the situation to heart. The workings of the Creative are complex and often unknowable. Slow progress will endure.

THIRD LINE Look not at the outward situation but at the effects of your own thoughts and actions. Through self-contemplation and self-correction you arrive at a proper understanding.

FOURTH LINE Those who understand proper principles will lead others with respect, tolerance, and gentleness.

FIFTH LINE It is a time for examining and correcting one's own attitudes. By contemplating the good you enable yourself to benefit from it.

SIXTH LINE The central truth is that one gains the world by becoming blameless. Sincere contemplation is the means to this end.

噬嗑

FIRE

THUNDER

21. SHIH HO/ BITING THROUGH

There is an obstacle to the expression of truth.
Withdrawal into quietness allows the Sage to moderate.

Unity has been broken by one who is not being true to proper principles. This may be another, or an element in one's own personality, or both. In any case, serious misfortune may result if the appropriate response is not made. The *I Ching* is very clear about what our proper action is when confronted with an obstacle of this nature: withdrawal into contemplation and a turning over of the matter to the Higher Power for resolution.

This is a time when aggressive action or intervention can only compound the misfortune. Use your strength to clearly separate yourself from incorrectness and realign yourself with the Sage. It is always our responsibility to acknowledge where something has gone wrong, but never our right to punish. The administration of justice is the sole province of the Deity.

The *I Ching* teaches us to forgive but not to forget. This does not mean one who reveals himself as inferior today should be regarded as such tomorrow. It means that we are wise to pay conscientious attention to the waxing and waning of truth in ourself and others. When truth predominates, we can progress. When it is eclipsed, we are obligated to withdraw and surrender the matter to the Sage.

FIRST LINE It is wise to learn from the first mistake. Repeating or persisting in it will compound the severity of the misfortune that follows it.

SECOND LINE The departure from truth is quite clear here. This may arouse anger and indignation. It is better to remain humble and balanced while the correction is carried out.

THIRD LINE This is an old and sticky issue. An attempt to punish will arouse hatred and resistance. In the end there is less trouble if one withdraws.

FOURTH LINE A correction is underway. Neither harshness nor careless relaxation is in order. Instead, persevere in a moderate and balanced fashion. The difficulties will be surmounted if you do so.

FIFTH LINE There is a temptation to be lenient. It may be too early to rejoin another or to take action. Remain gentle and watchful while the Creative corrects the situation.

SIXTH LINE An obstinate attitude results in an embarrassing and severe punishment. A return to humility and proper principles is the only means of escaping this.

賁

MOUNTAIN

FIRE

22. PI/ GRACE

Inside, the strength of simplicity and self-knowledge.
Outside, the beauty of acceptance and gentleness.

This hexagram encourages you to cultivate a quality of grace in your relationships and in your general way of being. In this way you gain a power greater than any other to open a way through obstructions in your dealings with others. Good fortune is yours if you concentrate on bringing more grace to your thoughts and actions now.

It is human nature to want to use forceful ways to try to get what we want from others and from life. Our egos encourage us to act aggressively, to speak boldly, to intimidate others, to "buffalo" our way through difficult situations. This false power can be momentarily satisfying to our ego, and temporary victories can be won in this way, but *genuine* power and *lasting* progress come from a different kind of strength altogether.

They come from inner strength, which is characterized by a steadfast devotion to the principles of humility, simplicity, equanimity, and acceptance. By gradually letting go of the vain, bullying energy of the ego and accepting the quiet guidance of the Higher Power, one acquires the substance that makes ongoing good fortune a possibility.

This is a time to relinquish self-important maneuvering. Instead, return to stillness and contemplate the inherent wisdom of the principles of the Sage. By practicing quiet strength within and gentle acceptance without, you acquire a grace that dissolves all barriers to progress.

FIRST LINE In the beginning, one must walk slowly and carefully. Do not assume that you know the answers or need to force a solution. Remain modest and allow the Unknown to guide you.

SECOND LINE Concern yourself not with the form things take but with their content. Cut through false appearances to determine whether your own strength or that of another is genuine or contrived.

THIRD LINE The situation appears positive. Do not relax into arrogance and indolence. Persevere in quiet correctness and good fortune is obtained.

FOURTH LINE There is a temptation to rely on false brilliance, advantage, or force. A return to modesty and innocence prevents misfortune.

FIFTH LINE Withdraw from the desires of your ego for luxury and recognition. Sincerity and simplicity are inevitably rewarded by the Sage.

SIXTH LINE By discarding the use of false power, one gains a view of the path to true power. In quiet acceptance there are a grace and a strength that overcome all else.

剝

MOUNTAIN

EARTH

23. PO/ SPLITTING APART

Do not attempt to intervene now.

A period has been entered when inferior influences will prevail. Even a superior person who seeks to act now will be undermined by the time. There is no reason to resist this state of affairs; indeed, it is natural that the inferior elements periodically come to the fore. Adversity is often a stimulant to our spiritual growth, and what is important is the spirit in which we meet it.

When challenging situations come to call, we are often overwhelmed with feelings of anxiety, doubt, and fear. We fear that if we do not act immediately and vigorously, we will be ruined; we doubt the power of the Creative to resolve the situation favorably. It is when we act upon these feelings that we engage in "splitting apart": we split apart from our spiritual path, our devotion to the Higher Power, and the wisdom of patient nonaction in the face of difficulty. If you take this course now, you will prevent the Creative from coming to your aid and unnecessarily increase your own misfortune.

The guide to proper behavior at such times lies in the image of the hexagram, which is "mountain over earth." By keeping as still and quiet as a mountain, by resting firmly on your foundation of proper principles, by accepting the nature of the time and not resisting it, you weather all storms. By trusting in nonaction, acceptance, and patience, you gain the strength of the very earth.

FIRST LINE Doubt and fear have propelled egos into action. Disaster results unless you abandon your grievances and agendas and allow the Creative to take over.

SECOND LINE Danger is all around you. If you are stubborn and unyielding you will be harmed. Use caution and wait for the Creative to come to your aid.

THIRD LINE Stay devoted to the superior person inside yourself. Though others may oppose you, no harm results.

FOURTH LINE The misfortune has reached its peak. Do not resist it any longer. Your energies should go toward correcting your attitude.

FIFTH LINE Through acceptance and self-correction you make possible a great change, like a vast school of fish instantly reversing its direction.

SIXTH LINE Evil feeds on evil and in time destroys everything connected with it. Cling to what is correct, and evil withers quickly away. Good fortune returns.

復

EARTH

THUNDER

24. FU / RETURN

A time of darkness comes to a close.

Receiving this hexagram is a sign that you have reached a turning point. This moment is akin to the winter solstice: the greatest adversity is past, and the light is beginning to return. Nonetheless, one cannot force the completion of the change, and it is wise to rest. Act only when you can move gently and innocently, and all will be well.

Fu also comes as a reminder to return to the light in yourself. Growth is only possible when we relinquish the expressions of the ego: pride, impatience, anger, and desire. To act forcefully or ambitiously now will only generate misfortune.

Let things develop naturally, in their own way. Simply observe and accept changes as you observe and accept the rising of the sun. Allow yourself to rest and gather strength for a time of growth ahead. By holding to modesty, gentleness, and correct conduct, you prepare the ground for a fruitful blossoming when the light fully returns.

FIRST LINE — Deviations from the path of good are inevitable. Misfortune is avoided when we put evil aside before it takes root.

SECOND LINE — There is danger of indulging in pride. Be tolerant of others and return to humbly following the good.

THIRD LINE — Fickle demands for immediate resolution slow your progress. Persevere quietly on the path of inner truth.

FOURTH LINE Depend not on your ambition or the opinion of others but on the principles of the Sage. For this you are rewarded.

FIFTH LINE The superior person avoids making excuses. Recognize errors, correct them, and there will be no misfortune.

SIXTH LINE A wrong attitude prevents the return to light. It is time for careful self-examination and self-correction. Opportunity wasted returns very slowly.

无妄

HEAVEN

THUNDER

25. WU WANG/ INNOCENCE (THE UNEXPECTED)

All good comes when we are innocent.

In the very center of each of us there dwells an innocent and divine spirit. If we allow ourselves to be guided by it in every situation, we can never go wrong. Wu Wang comes to remind us that we must actively disengage our egos before we can obtain the vast rewards that come from living in a state of innocence.

The nature of the ego is that when we exercise it, it takes us out of the present. When we engage in ambitions, anxieties, or anticipations, our ego is skipping ahead, and we miss the guidance of the Creative in the present moment. When we engage in anger, judgment, and condemnation—whether toward ourselves or others—our ego is looking backward, and we cannot see the Sage's clear solution to the present situation. In either case, the result is misfortune. Only by stilling the ego and accepting life in its entirety can we become innocent. In this state we are receptive to the help of the Higher Power and can meet with good fortune wherever we go.

You are advised now to stop looking forward and backward, to abandon your ambitions, to disengage from judgments and critical thinking. If a thought, attitude, or action is not in accord with the principles of acceptance, equanimity, humility, and gentleness, do not indulge in it. The *I Ching* encourages you to *actively practice innocence*. Because the ego is strong, you must make a conscious and conscientious effort to be innocent.

If you willfully unstructure your attitude, open your heart to the

Deity, and allow yourself to be guided by that which is innocent and pure, you will meet with success in the coming time.

FIRST LINE One who remains detached and innocent no matter what is assured of good fortune now.

SECOND LINE Do things for their own sake and not in anticipation of results. Attend to the path and not the goal, and all will be well.

THIRD LINE A misfortune comes that is not of your own making. Nevertheless, quiet acceptance is always the wisest response to the changes of life. Remain innocent or the misfortune is compounded.

FOURTH LINE Do not be swayed or persuaded by others. Stick to what you know to be innocent and correct.

FIFTH LINE If unexpected trouble comes, do not act against it. If you remain innocent and disengaged, it will pass quickly on its own.

SIXTH LINE If you are sincere in your efforts, but still no progress is made, simply return to acceptance. To attempt to force events is to abandon your innocence.

大畜

MOUNTAIN

HEAVEN

26. TA CH'U/ THE TAMING POWER OF THE GREAT

In the face of rising tension, keep still.
Honor in practice what you have learned from the I Ching.

A difficult and challenging time must be taken as an opportunity to express in the outer world our highest inner principles. This hexagram counsels us to keep still under pressure and embody the virtues of the *I Ching*. In this way even the most arduous trials can be successfully met.

Others are often tempted to test the inner strength that we have gained through study and discipline. By pushing and prodding they hope to reveal the weakness of our connection to truth. If we allow them to do this, we are undermined, and they go on, unlearning and satisfied at having engineered our downfall. On the other hand, if we keep still and cling firmly to what is right—the power of the great—then eventually we can tame the negative energy and instill in others the desire to grow spiritually.

It is just such challenges to our strength and character that enable us over time to embody in practice the strength of the *I Ching*. A spiritual understanding that is not practiced under fire is without value; only by applying our knowledge in trying situations do we come into genuine possession of it. So use these tests as opportunities to purify your thoughts and actions. By holding to what is correct in the face of pressure, you gain the strength and peace of mind of the spiritual masters.

If you deviate from the path of the Sage and act to punish or condemn others now, misfortune will result. Instead, meet attacks with stillness, acceptance, and fidelity to proper principles. Treat others with gentleness, patience, and forgiveness. If you are steadfast in this, good fortune will ultimately be yours.

FIRST LINE One wishes to advance aggressively against those who misbehave. Misfortune results. It is wise to endure the difficulty with restraint. In this way the resolution comes sooner.

SECOND LINE You cannot overcome the forces opposing you by struggling now. Accept this and still yourself. Self-discipline preserves your strength for use in a more beneficial time.

THIRD LINE A way opens to one who restrains his inferiors. By constantly renewing your humility, neutrality, and innocence you make steady gains.

FOURTH LINE It is futile to act out of strong emotions. Others will not be receptive. Still yourself and let the door open of its own accord.

FIFTH LINE The energy of desire is disruptive. Restrain this and hold to neutrality. In this way the situation is benefitted.

SIXTH LINE Obstacles are removed. Creative energy guided by humility and correctness meets with success.

頤

MOUNTAIN

THUNDER

27. I/THE CORNERS OF THE MOUTH (PROVIDING NOURISHMENT)

Give proper nourishment to yourself and others.

The image of this hexagram is that of an open mouth. It comes to remind us that the nourishment of our bodies and spirits is important and merits our conscientious attention.

The *I Ching* teaches us that if we wish to gauge someone's character, we should notice what he nourishes in himself and in others. Those who cultivate inferior behaviors and relationships are inferior people; those who cultivate superior qualities in themselves and others are superior people. This is a test that we should apply to ourselves as well as to others.

What you put into your body is obviously important. Because it determines your fundamental physical well-being, it is wise to be moderate and thoughtful about the food you eat. What you put into your mind is even more significant, and regulating it is a more subtle art. This hexagram gives us three-part advice on that subject.

The first counsel is that we should not feed our minds on desire. When we forego our equanimity and begin to desire something or someone, a host of other inferior influences comes into play: we become ambitious about obtaining the object of our desire; we become fearful that we will not; if we *do* achieve it our ego is gratified and strengthened and it soon issues another demand for us to meet. A self-reinforcing cycle of negativity is thus created. Therefore it is wise to hold yourself free from desire.

The second counsel is that we begin and continue in a regular practice of meditation. Sitting quietly with our eyes closed for even as little as ten or fifteen minutes a day begins to "clear the waste" out of our hearts and minds, making room for the nourishment of peace and wisdom to enter in. To sit in meditation is to tune your ear to the voice of the Sage, and it is the most powerful way of gaining his assistance.

The final counsel is that we observe tranquility in speech, thoughts, and actions. By cultivating calm and equanimity in all that you say, think, and do, you nourish your superior self and that of those around you. One who follows these three counsels now will meet with good fortune.

FIRST LINE — By engaging in doubt and envy you lose your independence. Sitting quietly in equanimity you are restored and uplifted.

SECOND LINE — If through laziness or weakness you are aligned with someone or something which is not correct, misfortune results. Consider this carefully.

THIRD LINE — The pursuit of desire and pleasure is "the nourishment that does not nourish." It is possible to throw one's entire life away in this fashion. On recognizing this, the superior person detaches himself and returns to the Sage.

FOURTH LINE — By nourishing yourself properly you gain stature and others are drawn to assist you. In this there is good fortune.

FIFTH LINE — You are weakened by the presence of an inferior element. Seek wise counsel and root this out before attempting further progress.

SIXTH LINE — One who truly emulates the Sage gains a position of great influence. If you lead others now as the Sage leads you, great things will be accomplished.

大過

LAKE

WIND

28. TA KUO / PREPONDERANCE OF THE GREAT

There are great pressures at work.
By meeting them with modesty and patience,
you avoid misfortune and meet with success.

The image of this hexagram is that of a beam under a great load: it sags in the middle and is in danger of giving way. You are in a similar situation now. The pressures of the moment are enormous, and there is a temptation to wriggle away and flee, or to resort to the plotting, conniving, and aggressive actions of the ego. It is by resisting this temptation and holding firmly to proper principles that you survive and succeed.

This is in fact a moment for which you have been preparing yourself for some time. A powerful energy has been accumulated—imagine a flood pressing against a dam—and it is up to you to direct its flow. If you succumb to fear, desire, or anger and resort to incorrect behaviors, the dam bursts and the pent-up energy causes destruction and misfortune. If, on the other hand, you cling to what is correct—modesty, balance, patience, independence, and gentleness—then you will obtain the aid of the Higher Power and the accumulated energy will be directed toward creating a profound success.

What is called for now is *quiet integrity*. With others, no matter how they may assault you, remain modest and patient. In your actions, seek to penetrate gently and steadily rather than forcibly and explosively. Meet the difficulties of the day cheerfully and resolutely. By taking great care now, by remaining correct in every moment, by embodying the principles of the Sage, you make possible the arrival of good fortune.

FIRST LINE Great care is required when one undertakes great projects. Lay your foundations with caution and proceed step by step.

SECOND LINE It is a time of renewal. Growth is possible if you remain modest and alert. Respect and honor those who are below you.

THIRD LINE It is a dangerous time and great care is required. Pushing ahead willfully leads to misfortune.

FOURTH LINE You gain the allegiance of others by holding to what is correct. Falling into self-importance leads to humiliation.

FIFTH LINE The foundation is incorrect. To neglect this is to assure one's own misfortune. A return to humility and neutrality reveals larger truths.

SIXTH LINE To pursue a goal without heeding what is correct brings misfortune. Sacrificing a personal aim in the interest of what is right honors the Sage. The most important and beneficial thing is always the furtherance of good, no matter the cost to oneself.

坎

WATER

WATER

29. K'AN/ THE ABYSMAL (WATER)

Flow like pure water
through difficult situations.

The image of the hexagram K'an is that of water: water falling from the heavens, water coursing over the earth in streams, water collecting itself in pure and silent pools. This image is meant to teach us how to conduct ourselves in trying situations. If we flow through them, staying true to what is pure and innocent in ourselves, we escape danger and reach a place of quiet refuge and good fortune beyond.

K'an often appears to warn of a troubling time either drawing near or already at hand, and to counsel you not to fall into longing for an immediate and effortless solution to the trouble. When you become "emotionally ambitious"—when you cling to comfort and desire to be free of the currents of change in life—you block the Creative from resolving difficulties in your favor. What is necessary now is to accept the situation, to flow with it like water, to remain innocent and pure and sincere while the Higher Power works out a solution.

It is not that you should not act now; it is that you should not act out of frustration, anxiety, despair, or a desire to escape the situation. Instead, still yourself and look for the lesson hidden inside the difficulty. Correct your attitude until it is open, detached, and unstructured. Abandon your goals and stay on the path, where you proceed step by step, arm in arm, with the Sage.

Those whose hearts and minds are kept pure and innocent relate properly to all events, understand their cosmic meaning, and flow through them with the strength, clarity, and brilliance of pure water.

FIRST LINE If you indulge a bad habit, no matter how small, eventually you fall into an abysmal pit. Leave behind incorrectness now.

SECOND LINE A dangerous abyss is open before you. This is a time for following the Sage cautiously and taking small, mindful steps.

THIRD LINE A step in any direction leads into danger. Do not act in any way. Disengage and strengthen your inner calm until a way through is clear.

FOURTH LINE A breakthrough comes if you look to the Sage for guidance. Sincerity in everything you think and say and do delivers you from danger.

FIFTH LINE Ambition leads to misfortune. If you will stop striving, the solution will come in the proper time.

SIXTH LINE If you persist in improper behavior when your heart knows what is correct, you will become hopelessly entangled in troubles. By following the good and remaining patient you save yourself and return to the light.

離

FIRE

FIRE

30. LI / THE CLINGING, FIRE

Cling to the power of higher truth.

It is in the nature of being human that we are dependent in many ways: dependent on water, air, and food for nourishment; dependent on shelter for warmth and protection; dependent on each other for family life and friendship. We are also spiritually dependent: when challenges arise, each of us must have some place to turn for guidance and support.

The image of the hexagram Li is that of fire clinging to the wood that it burns. Without a supply of fuel, there can be no fire. Likewise, a person without a source of spiritual sustenance cannot give off light in dark and challenging times.

Difficult situations tempt us to doubt the power of humility, acceptance, and correct behavior. We long to abandon our inner balance and lash out. It is just at such moments that it is most important to cling to what we know to be good and true and correct—like fire clings to the log it burns. By doing this we obtain the aid of the Higher Power.

You are advised to cling to proper principles now. Quietly, willingly, joyfully cling to what is superior in yourself; cling to the possibility of a positive outcome in the situation that faces you, no matter how unlikely it may seem; cling to the good in others, even when it is obscured by inferior influences; and cling to the power of the Deity to deliver truth where it is needed.

Trying times bring us the gift of showing where our devotion to proper principles ends. Deepen that devotion now, cling to truth and acceptance and independence, and you will meet with success.

FIRST LINE Do not hurry into things with incorrect thoughts or behaviors. By keeping yourself composed and correct at all times, you avoid misfortune.

SECOND LINE It is a time for moderation in every thing. Moderation of enthusiasm keeps you balanced. Moderation of despair deepens your understanding.

THIRD LINE Do not demand an end to one thing or a beginning to another. Accept that what is right comes in its own time. In this way you are always free.

FOURTH LINE A steady mind and heart meet with success. Be content to progress step by step. Worry and agitation only slow you down now.

FIFTH LINE A true change of heart is possible when we accept the necessity of adversity. Peace comes when we discontinue the strivings of the ego.

SIXTH LINE Inferior attitudes must be rooted out before progress can be made. Gently replace vanity and impatience with acceptance and modesty.

咸

LAKE

MOUNTAIN

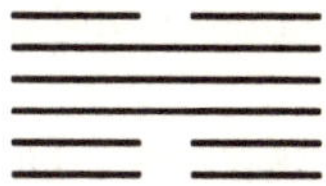

31. HSIEN/ INFLUENCE (WOOING)

An influence comes.
Good fortune to those
whose hearts are correct.

The hexagram Hsien indicates the coming of an influence. This may take the form of a teaching from the Sage, an interaction with another, or a disturbing or pleasing event. In any case, there is good fortune if you meet the influence with proper thoughts and actions.

It is a good time to remember that like attracts like. If one gives expression to higher things, then one is surrounded by higher things. If one indulges in what is inferior, then one can expect to have the company of inferiors. Therefore, it is wise to cling steadily to humility, independence, gentleness, and openness.

With others, keep an open heart, free of desire, condemning no one, enjoying affinities while retaining your equanimity. With the Sage, keep a clear connection. Seek resolutely to serve as a conduit for truth and innocence and goodness.

If the influence is challenging, persevere in correctness. If it is pleasing, also persevere in correctness. Maintaining your devotion to higher things insures success in the coming time.

FIRST LINE The toe is in the door. It is a good time to review your attitude and correct it if necessary. Only then can success arrive unhindered.

SECOND LINE Do not be seduced by appearances. True progress takes time, and much of the Sage's work is done away from our view, so be patient.

THIRD LINE Do not rush forward or allow yourself to be run over. Allow your quiet heart to lead you.

FOURTH LINE Abandon ambitions, anxieties, and agendas. What is necessary and worthwhile arises from the stillness within.

FIFTH LINE Adaptability is advisable. Avoid pushing or chasing others. There is no remorse if you listen carefully to the Sage.

SIXTH LINE Express your knowledge in your conduct rather than in your words. Trust the wisdom of the Sage and allow each person to come to his own understanding.

恒

THUNDER

WIND

32. HÊNG / DURATION

Remain steady and allow the world to shape itself.

Receiving this hexagram is an encouragement to endure, to move ahead by abiding in what is true and correct. It is not a time to let the ego swell with successes nor to despair at misfortunes. It is simply a time to hold to the path of essential truth.

It is likely that a change has occurred, or is about to. It is your responsibility to hold your course and go on without regarding this change. Constancy in correct thought and action is the order of the day. Rather than letting your head be turned, simply hold steady on your spiritual path while the world reforms around you.

Do not indulge in judgment, impatience, or ambitious thinking now. By concerning yourself only with what is essential and true and good, only with what is in front of you and your correct relationship to it, you meet with good fortune now.

FIRST LINE — Do not expect too much too soon. That which is worthwhile is created slowly and carefully.

SECOND LINE — Be mindful of the machinations of the ego. Do not strive, boast, or despair. Return quietly to inner strength and quietude.

THIRD LINE — There is danger of being swayed by external circumstances. To measure or compare is to depart from the path and invite misfortune.

FOURTH LINE That which is sought in an incorrect fashion is never obtained. Concentrate on your attitude rather than your goals.

FIFTH LINE It is not our responsibility to control or direct others. Allow them their own path, and keep to yours. If the paths meet, fine. If they do not, also fine.

SIXTH LINE Do not become restless for constant change. Allow the Sage to work in his own way. "Taking over" brings a fall.

遯

HEAVEN

MOUNTAIN

33. TUN/RETREAT

This is a time for disengagement and retreat.
In stillness you are out of the reach of danger.

It is inherent in the design of life that forces of darkness and disruption come into prominence from time to time. This hexagram indicates that this is such a time and advises you to respond by quietly retreating. To struggle or resist in anger now is to add fuel to the fire of negativity which threatens to consume you.

The superior person accepts that there is a natural ebb and flow between the forces of light and dark in the world. Wisdom lies not in resisting these movements but in responding to them appropriately. Just as a plant which sprouts in the dead of winter is doomed, and one which sprouts in spring flourishes, so it is with us. Success and prosperity accrue to those who advance in times of light and retreat in times of darkness. To retreat now is to benefit, in the end, from the changing tides.

Retreat is not the same thing as surrender, capitulation, or abandonment, which are desperate and unsatisfying measures. Neither is it characterized by a hardening into angry or punitive emotions. It is instead an acceptance and a choice: we calmly accept that the energies of the moment are against us, and we wisely choose to withdraw into the safety of stillness. In this dignified and balanced manner we protect ourselves from negative influences and arrive rested in a more beneficial hour.

FIRST LINE — You linger in an involvement with a negative force. Do not allow your ego to draw you into misfortune. Disengage completely and enter into stillness.

SECOND LINE — One cries out for a just resolution. This can only come if we quietly observe proper principles. Avoid placing demands on the universe, and success will come.

THIRD LINE — The clamorings of the ego interfere with your retreat. This invites a humiliation. Devote yourself to quiet truth, not to emotional struggle.

FOURTH LINE — To compete and struggle only strengthens the determination of the opposing forces. If you disengage and balance yourself they have nothing to push against.

FIFTH LINE — Be friendly but firm when the time has come to retreat. Determination to behave correctly prevents you from being seduced into damaging intrigues.

SIXTH LINE — When one cheerfully accepts the necessity of retreat, the path becomes easy and clear.

大壯

THUNDER

HEAVEN

34. TA CHUANG/THE POWER OF THE GREAT

To achieve true power and true greatness one must be in harmony with what is right.

False power and false greatness can be seen all around us in the world. Through egotistical and aggressive manipulations many people obtain a temporary position of influence. The *I Ching* teaches us a different way of acquiring and using power, one that leads to true greatness and enduring influence. The way of the Sage unites power with modesty, justice, gentleness, and equanimity.

The hexagram Ta Chuang indicates that you have increased your power now by purifying your thoughts and actions. Through contemplation of higher principles you have begun to open doors for yourself; through alignment with what is true and good you gain insight into situations and the power to resolve them in your favor. But it is important to remember that it is the Sage who is the source of your strength. If your ego takes over and wields the power that is at hand, the ensuing misfortune will be great.

The *I Ching* counsels us not to misuse our strength by judging, condemning, punishing, manipulating, or dismissing others. It advises reticence in speech and action: more often than not, the truly superior person relies on stillness and nonaction, allowing inner truth to penetrate gently to the heart of difficulties. The *I Ching* also cautions us to wait patiently for the appropriate time for speech or action. Power can make us eager, but eagerness unbalances and leads us into trouble. By listening carefully and patiently to the Sage we know when to move ahead, when to wait, and when to retreat.

In the end, true greatness comes only to those in whom strength and proper principles are firmly united. If you follow the Sage and persevere steadfastly in what is correct, you will inherit the power of the great.

FIRST LINE Your power is being directed by your ego now. Detach, disengage, and restore your equanimity, or there will be humiliation.

SECOND LINE The resistance begins to give way and progress is possible now. Exuberant self-confidence will lead you to ruin. By remaining modest and gentle you find your way to good fortune.

THIRD LINE He who butts against things does damage to his own head. The superior person avoids using his strength rashly and goes forward only when the way is open.

FOURTH LINE If you work quietly and steadily at removing obstacles, you meet with success in the end. Allow the correctness of your thoughts and actions to speak for you now.

FIFTH LINE One who gives up a stubborn and harsh way of acting will not regret it. No harm comes if you soften now.

SIXTH LINE The obstinate use of power entangles you further instead of freeing you from difficulty. If you notice this and correct yourself, all will be well.

晋

FIRE

EARTH

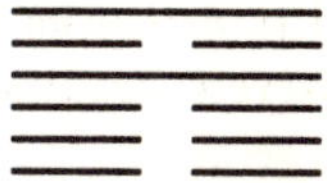

35. CHIN/ PROGRESS

You progress like the rising sun.
The brighter your virtue, the higher you rise.

This hexagram announces a time of significant and easy progress. Your influence and understanding grow by leaps and bounds as long as you maintain your alliance with the Sage, for it is from that alliance that the current progress springs. The only limit to growth now is your devotion to higher things: if this is true and complete and steady, there will be great gains now.

The image of the hexagram is that of the sun rising over the earth. To our view, the further it moves away from darkness, the higher the sun rises. The same is true of us: the extent to which we progress is determined by how far we distance ourselves from inferior influences.

It is important, when success comes, not to fall into the traps of the ego: taking credit for gains, resting on laurels, indulging in desires, or plotting toward ambitions. The superior person instead uses times of progress to brighten his virtue, recognizing that it was his commitment to proper principles that brought success in the first place.

Continue to purify your thoughts, attitudes, and conduct now. The greatest power in this beneficial time accrues to those who serve the Higher Power in every moment.

FIRST LINE In spite of correct behavior, you are not confident of progress. Simply continue to quietly do what is right. In this way success is assured.

SECOND LINE Progress may be halted because another fails to help. Persevere in humility and correctness. A union grounded in proper principles bears fruit in time.

THIRD LINE Do not bemoan your own weaknesses. Simply stay on the path as steadily as you can, and like-minded others will assist you.

FOURTH LINE In times of great progress there is a danger of expanding the ego. Do not amass luxuries or wield power self-righteously. Misfortune comes to those who abandon humility and correct conduct in good times.

FIFTH LINE Do not concern yourself with each little gain or loss. The greatest influence comes not through aggressive action but through remaining detached and devoted to the good in all things.

SIXTH LINE Harshness against others brings not progress but misfortune. Aggressiveness is permissible only in eliminating one's own inferior tendencies.

明夷

EARTH

FIRE

36. MING I / DARKENING OF THE LIGHT

Darkness reigns in the external world now.
Disengage from negative feelings and
maintain your inner light.

This is a time when darkness and inferior energies surround you. The image is that of the sun completely swallowed by the earth. The only light left is that inside your own heart, and you are counseled to return to it, maintain it, and quietly nourish yourself with it.

It is in dark moments that a correct attitude is most important. If we fight against the darkness, we are swallowed by it and suffer great misfortune. If we react to the lack of visible progress with despair and negativity, we extinguish our own inner light and block the aid of the Creative. If we try to persuade others that they must return to the light, we exhaust ourselves in vain now.

In a time such as this, it is wise to adopt a stance of outer disengagement and inner perseverance. Do not focus on or interact with the negative influences around you; this only strengthens their grip on you. Step aside, yield, let go, allow people and events to pass without attachment. Direct your attention inside, to *your* inner light, *your* devotion to what is right, *your* conversation with the Higher Power.

Progress may be slow, but there will indeed be progress. Remember that much of the work of the Higher Power is hidden from us, and that we enable and assist it by remaining detached, accepting, and reserved in the face of negative influences.

FIRST LINE Your ego is unsatisfied with the path of correctness. However, to strive out of desire or despair will bring misfortune. Cling to what is calm and good no matter what others do, and allow the Creative to work in its own time.

SECOND LINE You have been wounded by a dark force. You can heal yourself by healing others around you who are in need. This brings good fortune.

THIRD LINE Just because we recognize the source of the problem does not mean that it will disappear immediately. Perseverance in truth and correctness dissolves the influence in time.

FOURTH LINE What you recognize to be inferior you must immediately leave behind. Lingering with negativity invites a disaster now.

FIFTH LINE An external darkness cannot be escaped now. You are wise to yield outwardly while maintaining strength and purpose within.

SIXTH LINE The darkness has reached a climax. If you are firm in holding to acceptance, balance, and correctness, you will emerge successful.

家人

WIND

FIRE

37. CHIA JÊN / THE FAMILY (THE CLAN)

A healthy family, a healthy country,
a healthy world—all grow outward
from a single superior person.

The hexagram Chia Jên concerns the proper foundation of human communities. The *I Ching* teaches that all clans must have a superior person at their center if they are to prosper and succeed. Therefore, in order to improve our family, company, nation, or world community, we must begin by improving ourselves.

If you will observe healthy families you will always see present in them three qualities: love, faithfulness, and correctness. When we truly love others, we are naturally kind, gentle, and patient with them. When we are faithful to others, we place proper principles and conduct above temporary influences like anger, desire, or greed. And when we practice correctness, we spiritually nourish ourselves and all those around us. When all three qualities are cultivated, a healthy clan springs naturally into being.

The difference between paying lip service to these ideals and practicing them is profound. If you advocate high ideals and actions to others but do not embody them yourself, your influence will disintegrate for lack of a proper foundation. Therefore, in order to inspire superior qualities in others, you must first instill them in yourself.

Concentrate not upon influencing others or external events but upon strengthening your inner devotion to proper principles. When modesty, acceptance, equanimity, and gentleness become deeply ingrained in your character, they will flow steadily outward from you.

Soon you will find yourself enmeshed in a web of healthy relationships, and in this there is great good fortune.

FIRST LINE There must be firmness if relationships are to succeed. If we give in to the demands and tantrums of the ego, there is misfortune. We prosper when we meet others halfway—no more and no less.

SECOND LINE Do not seek to influence through force or aggressive actions. Instead, penetrate gently by holding correct thoughts.

THIRD LINE Harshness leads you to misfortune, and so does spinelessness. Only by being gentle without and strong within will you succeed.

FOURTH LINE Well-being is a by-product of inner balance, acceptance, and conscientious conduct. Concentrate on cultivating these now.

FIFTH LINE If one's character is good, then one's influence will be felt. By disengaging from inferiors we increase our power.

SIXTH LINE If you are resolutely correct in thought as well as action, there will be good fortune. The power of inner truth and goodness draws others and the Creative to our side.

睽

FIRE

LAKE

38. K'UEI/ OPPOSITION

Misunderstanding truth creates opposition.

There are many occasions in life which tempt us into negative thoughts. Anxiety about the future, mistrust of another person, bodily pain, fear of failure or even success—all of these tempt us into mistrusting life and believing that life is against us. When we fall into this trap, we are in opposition to the workings of the Creative and success becomes impossible.

The simple truth is that every moment in every person's life contains the teaching he or she most needs at that time. It is not always immediately apparent why a thing is happening because the Sage is often inclined to work in a roundabout fashion. Nonetheless, whatever is happening now is what *must* happen. Our only task is to trust the process and allow the lesson to seep in.

This hexagram comes as a signal that you are resisting life and preventing your own progress. Nonetheless, success is still possible, for every opposition carries within it the seeds of agreement. Cease resisting yourself, others, life, the Sage. Let go of dark thoughts and aggressive actions. By returning to acceptance, neutrality, and devotion to the way of the Sage, you dissolve the opposition within yourself and open the way for understanding and good fortune to arrive.

FIRST LINE Do not try to create unity by force. Meet every situation halfway and remain correct.

SECOND LINE Opposition hinders a meeting of the minds. An open and unstructured approach is best. Often an answer arrives accidentally.

THIRD LINE Everything appears to conspire against you. Meet this test with balance and acceptance, and a good end will come.

FOURTH LINE Mistrust of fate leaves you isolated and alone. By rejoining the path of the Sage, you return to joy.

FIFTH LINE A misunderstanding cloaks the truth. Look beyond appearances and a productive relationship is gained.

SIXTH LINE Neither life, the Sage, nor your companions seek to harm you. Lay aside mistrust and release the tensions of the moment.

蹇

WATER

MOUNTAIN

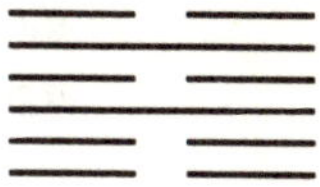

39. CHIEN/ OBSTRUCTION

Surrounded by obstructions, one must first retreat, then seek the direction of the Sage.

There is an old saying which fits this hexagram: "You are caught between a rock and a hard place." In other words, you are surrounded by obstructions. As much as you may want to blame others for the difficulty, in all likelihood the true obstruction is in your own thinking. What is called for now is a retreat into self-examination and self-correction.

Emotions of desire, fear, or anger may tempt you to take action now, but do not be seduced. The presence of these strong feelings is proof that you are off balance and need to steady yourself. As long as you try to forcibly achieve external results—rather than carefully following higher truth step by step—you will be obstructed from making personal progress.

Whenever we indulge in judgments about others, we obstruct our own peace of mind and progress. We should choose instead to see the best in others, allow them to come and go as they will, and turn our energies inward, toward self-improvement.

Often the faults in our own thinking are revealed only with the aid of others. You would be wise now to seek the advice of a qualified counselor or truth-minded friend. Retreat, self-examination, and self-correction will remove the obstructions that block your path now.

FIRST LINE Do not resist difficulties or advance against them. By retreating and observing, you learn an important lesson. Then moving forward becomes easy.

SECOND LINE You are not to blame for the current difficulties. Neither should you concern yourself with penalizing others. Accept, let go of judgments, and simply do what is correct.

THIRD LINE Do not act recklessly and egotistically. Retreat and restore your equanimity, and good fortune results.

FOURTH LINE By keeping still you gather the resources you need to progress. The way will be shown when the time is right, and not before.

FIFTH LINE The obstructions can only be overcome by the strength of proper principles. Through perseverance and correctness you obtain the aid you need to succeed.

SIXTH LINE Do not turn your back when you are needed. The superior person exercises his higher nature now, saving not only himself but others around him.

解

THUNDER

WATER

40. HSIEH/ DELIVERANCE

A change in attitude
delivers you from difficulties.

The hexagram Hsieh signals the beginning of a deliverance from danger, tensions, and difficulty. The *I Ching* instructs you here on both the cause of deliverance and how you must act in order to fully benefit from it.

Deliverance is always caused by a change in our attitude. The Higher Power uses conflicts and obstacles to teach us lessons that we refuse to learn in an easier way, but they only darken our doorstep until we have acknowledged the lesson. So long as we ignore or resist difficulty it remains our constant companion; as soon as we accept its presence as a sign that some self-correction is needed, our deliverance begins. Truly, the only way to dispel trouble and regain peace of mind is to change our attitude.

The *I Ching* also teaches us that we have several responsibilities once our deliverance begins. The first is to forgive the misdeeds of others. The image of the hexagram is that of a powerful rainstorm washing away what is unclean. This, then, is a time to clean every slate and begin anew, meeting others halfway with gentleness and patience.

Next, we are advised to restore our inner balance and see that it is maintained. Deliverance offers us a return to equanimity, and we must avail ourselves of the opportunity conscientiously. Finally, we are counseled not to try to force progress, even though the time is beneficial. If we have truly changed our attitude, we have become detached, innocent, modest, and accepting. In this state we allow progress to unfold naturally according to the will of the Sage.

FIRST LINE The obstacle is overcome. By keeping quiet and still you insure that another does not arise.

SECOND LINE Ideas that flatter our egos prevent deliverance. Through devotion to what is correct they are removed and the way is cleared for good fortune.

THIRD LINE There is a temptation when we are delivered from trouble to become proud and hold ourselves above others. If you indulge in this, a humiliating fall results.

FOURTH LINE Free yourself from inferior influences, both in your self and in your acquaintances. Otherwise there is no room for the superior to enter your life.

FIFTH LINE To truly be free of inferior influences you must firmly break with them in your own mind. Until this inner disengagement is complete, no external action will remove them.

SIXTH LINE The ego prevents deliverance by holding on to an incorrect attitude. By sincerely seeking the help of the Sage you can root this out and become free.

損

MOUNTAIN

LAKE

41. SUN/DECREASE

Be still, lessen the power of the ego, and misfortune will be avoided.

It is a fact of life that times of decrease come upon us: our resources are limited, difficulty surrounds us, and our egos generate angry and unhappy emotions. Nonetheless, such times are good for us. If we respond to them by quieting our egos and turning sincerely to the Higher Power for help, we emerge from the period of decrease stronger, healthier, and wiser.

When we discover that we are unable to achieve our goals, our egos become infuriated. We are tempted to harden into anger and bitterness, to lash out, to desperately and aggressively grab for control over the situation. If we do this, however, we only push our own salvation further away.

The *I Ching* counsels a withdrawal into stillness now. The image is that of a spring reverting to the inside of the mountain during a time of drought. By returning to its quiet center during the time of decrease, it avoids evaporating and exhausting itself in vain. You would be wise to follow this example. To try to force progress by arguing, manipulating, or making excuses will only bring your own downfall. Instead, disengage from your inferior elements—however passionately they seek expression—and turn to the Sage for guidance and assistance.

The hexagram Sun issues a call to sacrifice negative feelings, accept the powerlessness of the ego against the currents of life, and return to contemplation of the principles of the Sage. In stillness and meditation we enrich the higher parts of ourselves and thus bring an end to the time of decrease.

FIRST LINE Give aid to others where you can do so with a proper attitude: without seeking recognition, and without unbalancing them. Strive to have a gentle and detached influence.

SECOND LINE To truly help others, you must maintain your own dignity. Everyone is decreased if you indulge in what is inferior.

THIRD LINE By relinquishing an inferior element you make room for a superior one. The Deity arrives when we disengage our egos and ask for his help.

FOURTH LINE By correcting your bad habits and cultivating innocence, you draw others to you. Good fortune is widespread.

FIFTH LINE Nothing can prevent success from coming to those who follow the good, the true, and the innocent at every turn.

SIXTH LINE Through stillness and innocence one gains an increase. Be generous and benevolent with others and still greater increases will follow.

益

WIND

THUNDER

42. I/INCREASE

Powerful improvements are underway.

The coming of the hexagram I signifies a period of increase when the power of heaven descends to surround and invigorate our lives. Like all phases, this too will come to an end, but if "we make hay while the sun shines," tremendous progress can be made at this time.

It is in the nature of human beings to relax and become careless when things begin to go well. The *I Ching* teaches us that we should not do this if we desire the fullest blessings of the beneficial hour. Indeed, our rewards are multiplied if we increase our conscientiousness in auspicious times, rather than decrease it. There are two ways in which the *I Ching* especially encourages us to do this.

Our first task is to make sacrifices for others. In all of your interactions now, embody generosity in thought and action. Forgive what is inferior in others and seek out the good. By giving, encouraging, and assisting, you will draw the superior person in everyone into devoted action.

Your second task in this time of increase is to go on strengthening yourself "as thunder and wind strengthen each other." This means that if you see something good in another, you imitate it, and when you discover something inferior in yourself, you eliminate it.

These simple practices, if continued conscientiously over time, will improve your character and fortunes immeasurably. Through service and self-improvement you assure yourself of great progress in the days ahead.

FIRST LINE Your own good fortune makes it possible for you to do a great deed. Through selflessness and a sense of purpose you can accomplish much now.

SECOND LINE If you sincerely love the good and true, and you pursue them at every turn, nothing will prevent you from achieving your aims.

THIRD LINE Even difficult situations can enrich you if you are correct in relating to them. Quietly follow the path of inner truth.

FOURTH LINE This is a time when a wise intermediary can be of great help. Follow the example of the Sage and assist others sincerely.

FIFTH LINE True kindness is expressed not in hope of recognition but in hope of helping another. It is because of this that it is inevitably recognized.

SIXTH LINE If we do not help those below us, we weaken our own foundation. Times of increase only continue if we remain generous, balanced, and correct throughout.

夬

43. KUAI/BREAKTHROUGH (RESOLUTENESS)

A breakthrough. Do not be drawn back into bad habits.

The arrival of the hexagram Kuai indicates that a long-awaited change is at hand. A difficulty that has oppressed you over a long period is now about to dissolve. It is important to respond in the proper way.

There is a temptation on obtaining relief to fall into the traps of the ego: pride at having dispersed the trouble, self-righteousness about having triumphed through correctness, anger at one who we think was the source of the problem, or a desire to remain free of all difficulty in the future. None of these responses is appropriate to the situation at hand.

What is needed now is *resoluteness*: a firm commitment to continuing the battle for good and to the self-examination that makes all good things possible. This is not a time to lapse back into negative mental habits and enjoy the "vacation" provided by the breakthrough. Do not rest on your laurels, but push forward, deepening your inner strength and your resistance to the influence of inferiors, both in yourself and others. Strengthen those around you by setting an example of self-improvement and self-correction. Great progress and good fortune are available now to one who makes proper use of the opening.

FIRST LINE Resistance is still present. Go forward only as far as you can travel in a spirit of calm and equanimity. Ignore demands of the ego to triumph or resolve everything at once.

SECOND LINE Remain watchful for unanticipated dangers at all times. Thus you are never surprised and can greet any event with poise and readiness.

THIRD LINE The situation attempts to provoke you to act. Do not be drawn in. Do nothing until a quiet sense of truth is established.

FOURTH LINE Restlessness encourages you to force your will on the situation. This brings misfortune. Allow yourself to be led like a quiet lamb by the shepherd of inner truth.

FIFTH LINE If it is your habit to indulge in what is inferior, break your habit now. Persevere in what is right, accept life, and you will succeed.

SIXTH LINE The situation seems resolved but may not be. Only a steady devotion to correct behavior brings the desired completion.

姤

HEAVEN

WIND

44. KOU/ COMING TO MEET

Darkness reappears unexpectedly.
Caution and reticence are in order.

It is a dangerous hour. Through an eruption of our inferior nature darkness has interrupted the flow of light. The inferior can be quite seductive, and if we are not resolute in resisting it, the moment can be lost to misfortune.

In one's self, this is a time to examine motives; those which are of questionable honor should be uprooted and discarded. Be wary of situations that engage your ego and tempt you into anger, self-righteousness, or desire. Actively employ your higher nature to test the correctness of tempting ideas and circumstances; that which seems suspicious almost certainly is.

In your conduct with others, practice modesty, independence, and patience with great discipline. Avoid anger or arrogance at all costs; withdraw whenever you cannot meet another in a balanced and independent way. Neither encourage another to forego his balance nor indulge him if he does so. Again, withdraw into stillness if the circumstances indicate the presence of inferior influences. Reticence and self-scrutiny are the order of the day.

FIRST LINE The time to control the inferior is in the beginning. Whatever negative emotion seeks expression now should be reined in before it builds momentum. Use your will to return to balance.

SECOND LINE A dark impulse clings. Do not resist it with violence. Simply decline to express it and wait patiently, concentrating on what is correct, until it passes.

THIRD LINE The temptation is to argue one's case. This will only serve to beckon misfortune. Observe the urge but do not indulge it.

FOURTH LINE Others may give expression to inferior qualities. There is no merit in judging, condemning, or correcting them. Tolerance and a gentle hand are advised, no matter how offensive the difficulty.

FIFTH LINE Do not use your own poise and principles to berate another. Trust that whatever is true and good in you will transform others' inferior elements without forceful effort on your part. Gentleness brings success.

SIXTH LINE Constant challenges from inferior qualities, either your own or someone else's, may necessitate a withdrawal. Simply remain mindful of your connection to the Sage and tolerate accusations or unpleasantness with equanimity and restraint.

萃

LAKE
EARTH

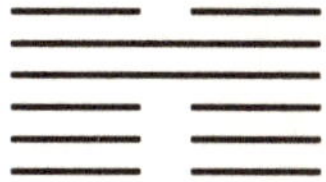

45. TS'UI/GATHERING TOGETHER

To lead others toward the good,
one must purify one's own character.

The *I Ching* teaches that the world cannot move toward harmony and well-being unless human beings act in unison to further what is good and true. Our power as individuals is multiplied when we gather together as families, groups, and communities with common goals. It is our *collective* strength that makes positive change possible in the world. However, the tremendous power of human collectives must be directed by a qualified leader. The hexagram Ts'ui encourages you to develop your character into that of a leader.

Before a person may gather others together to achieve good, he must first gather together within himself proper principles. A leader who is not balanced and collected within himself will always be suspected by his followers, and in the hour when he needs them most, they will hesitate. Therefore the first task of the potential leader is to accumulate in his own character all that is good and true and correct.

In a very real sense the progress of the world depends upon your progress as an individual now. Concentrate, then, on examining and correcting your thoughts, attitudes, and actions. Improve yourself into the kind of person you yourself would follow wholeheartedly and without hesitation. Learn to accept the natural progress that occurs when you act in harmony with proper principles, and seek no progress at the expense of those principles. Train yourself to avoid misfortunes by anticipating them in advance.

By purifying your character in this way and clinging steadfastly to higher things, you lead yourself and others toward well-being and good fortune.

FIRST LINE Those who hesitate in what is correct lose the way. Do not allow your ego to become aroused now. Stay centered in humility, acceptance, and innocence and you will meet with success now.

SECOND LINE Allow yourself and others to be guided by inner truth. Those who belong together will come together naturally. Be sincere and let the Creative do the work.

THIRD LINE One who is humiliated and isolated would like to reunite. Generosity, tolerance, and reliance on the Sage heal all wounds in time.

FOURTH LINE If you work for the good unselfishly now, you will be overrun with success and good fortune.

FIFTH LINE Some who gather together may not be sincere about doing what is right. Do not become engaged with inferior influences. The way to bring others into unison is to steadily improve yourself.

SIXTH LINE Genuine progress is only made if we are sincere in our devotion to the Sage. There will be cause for lament if we are not.

升

EARTH

WIND

46. SHÊNG/ PUSHING UPWARD

Activity grounded in truth
brings progress and good fortune.

It is a time when great progress can be made through effort of will. However, it is essential that all your activity be characterized by humility, conscientiousness, and adaptability. Progress as a tree does, bending around obstacles rather than confronting them, pushing upward steadily but gently.

There is nothing to be feared from others now. Feel free to ask for help from those who are in a position to give it. Be neither subservient nor forceful with those you encounter; simply meet everyone with tolerance and gentle goodwill. Those who look for the good in others find it there.

If fears or doubts intrude, remain quietly focused on the activity at hand. Cultivate inner independence and trust the leadership of the Sage. The time is ripe for progress if you put forth an effort that is innocent, sincere, and balanced.

FIRST LINE As above, so below. The confidence needed to push upward is found not in our egos but in our relationship with the Sage.

SECOND LINE A goal may be reached but only if one's character is fully aligned with proper principles. It is always more important to maintain humility and equanimity than to satisfy an ambition.

THIRD LINE All barriers to progress are removed. The degree of success will be determined by the closeness of your alliance with the Sage.

FOURTH LINE Success is attained as a result of your careful attention to self-examination and self-improvement.

FIFTH LINE Progress is made in steps, not in leaps. Move only as far as the opening allows. Remain neutral and tolerant of adversity. When in doubt, remain still.

SIXTH LINE Disengage ego and ambition. Do not hurl yourself at a closed door. Inner independence is your most valuable asset.

困

LAKE

WATER

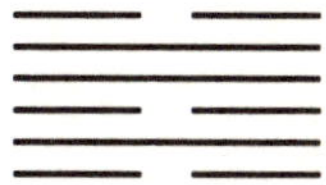

47. K'UN/OPPRESSION (EXHAUSTION)

An unavoidable time of adversity.
Quiet strength insures a later success.

It is a time of oppression and exhaustion. None of us escapes such moments; they are simply a part of living. By meeting them in the correct spirit and cheerfully bending instead of breaking, you weather the adversity and meet with success at a later time.

Inferior elements, either in one's self, another, or the larger world, interfere now to restrain the superior person. It is foolish to fight against the restraint; success is simply not possible now. Rid yourself of the desire to progress and return to neutrality and acceptance. The stubborn pursuit of results will bring misfortune.

With others, quietness and equanimity are the watchwords of the moment. Say little, and say it gently. A similar reticence and gentleness should be applied to yourself. Do not lapse into impatience or mistrust of the Deity. Accept that the Creative often works in a way that we cannot see or understand.

A feeling of despair or depression is a sign that you are holding a false belief. To perpetuate an untruth about yourself, another, or the Sage is to block your own happiness. Root out and remove any idea or attitude which causes negative feelings.

By opening your mind, quieting your heart, and calmly holding to proper principles, you make it possible for the Creative to eliminate the oppression that currently exists.

FIRST LINE The situation must be met inside one's self. Allowing despair to take over prevents resolution. Work to have a balanced, cheerful, and accepting attitude.

SECOND LINE Your heart feels exhausted. If so, it is impatience and ambition that exhaust it. Actively note your blessings, concentrate on inner truth, and allow the Higher Power to renew your strength.

THIRD LINE Restless effort undermines one's interests. It is unwise to charge repeatedly at a closed door. Withdraw into stillness and accept both the challenges and the blessings of the day.

FOURTH LINE Fixed ideas and a hardened mind are poison. Let go of judgment—including that which is directed at yourself—and turn to the Sage for help.

FIFTH LINE Even a superior person is oppressed now. Modesty and reliance on quiet truth preserve you in this difficult hour.

SIXTH LINE The difficulty is coming to a close, but only if one is firm against harshness, doubt, and despair. Help only comes where there is room for it to enter.

井

WATER

WIND

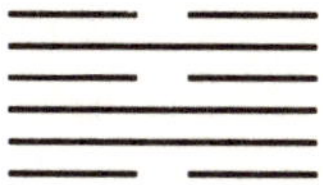

48. CHING/THE WELL

Return to the well of goodness.

No community can survive without a dependable source of pure water. In a similar way, human beings cannot survive without a reliable source of spiritual nourishment. In fact, we need *two* wells: an external source of guidance, such as the *I Ching*, and an internal source of guidance, which must be our own good character. This hexagram comes to encourage you to concentrate on developing, purifying, and utilizing your two "wells."

Notice the name of this hexagram: "Ching/The Well." The *I Ching* has survived in countless civilizations for thousands of years for a simple reason: it is an inexhaustible source of spiritual nourishment. It provides us with the fundamental building blocks of a successful life. If you approach it sincerely, without mistrust or frivolity, it will guide you through every difficult hour with unimpeachable wisdom. If you muddy the well, however, by doubting the *I Ching* or by placing your ego desires above the counsel it gives you, you impede your own progress.

The purest of external wells, the *I Ching* is also an invaluable aid in developing and cleansing the internal well of your own good character. It will, if you are sincere, reveal to you the fundamental issues of your life, and it will instill in you the values necessary to successfully negotiate those issues.

The hexagram Ching comes to encourage you not to muddy the well of your good character in any way now. In relating to others, look beyond any external faults or "muddiness" and acknowledge the clear well that exists somewhere inside them. No person is without this, and by speaking to it you strengthen it. If you will follow these counsels, you will meet with a true and lasting success in life.

FIRST LINE If you throw away proper principles, the well is muddied and no one can be nourished. Be patient with others and concentrate on correct behavior.

SECOND LINE If one has good qualities but neglects them, he breaks the jug and cannot draw from the well. Let go of arrogance and stay on the path of the Sage.

THIRD LINE Your well is clean but you do not drink from it: you understand what is right, but you avoid it. Draw on the strength of the Sage and correct this.

FOURTH LINE The well is in need of lining. Work must be done in the background before the desired result can be achieved.

FIFTH LINE One must not only draw the water from the well but also drink it. Wisdom that is not put to practical use is meaningless.

SIXTH LINE Inner wealth consists of modesty, balance, understanding, and compassion for others. When you have achieved this, your outer fortune will be unlimited.

革

49. KO/ REVOLUTION

Devotion to truth enables a revolution.

The hexagram Ko announces the arrival of a time of revolution. A set of conditions, internal or external or both, is ready to pass away in favor of a more beneficial situation. What enables this transformation is your conscious and vigorous adherence to correct thought and behavior.

No revolution in outer things is possible without a prior revolution in one's inner way of being. Whatever change you aspire to in your affairs must be preceded by a change in heart, an active deepening and strengthening of your resolve to meet every event with equanimity, detachment, and innocent goodwill. When this spiritual poise is achieved within, magnificent things are possible without.

The revolutions of others are enabled also when we refine the fire of goodness and truth inside ourselves. Sincere commitment to higher things travels outward in powerful waves from the superior person, and all those around are affected by this. Indisputably, to lead one's inner self to truth and peace is to lead the outer world to truth and peace. A beneficial revolution is assured to one who takes this path now.

FIRST LINE Perseverance in innocent nonaction bears the greatest fruit at this time. Wait in humility and quiet restraint for a clear way to open.

SECOND LINE A revolution is possible if one first prepares the ground. Strengthen your humility and still your ego before, during, and after taking action.

THIRD LINE Do not be hasty; neither should you hesitate excessively. Act with perseverance and gentleness when it becomes clear that the time is right.

FOURTH LINE Great changes are only possible if your inner attitude is blameless. That which is not just will not last.

FIFTH LINE People instinctively understand and support a revolution brought by one who is completely aligned with higher principles.

SIXTH LINE That which is inferior takes time to transform completely. Accept small gains as steady progress and continually reaffirm your devotion to the path of the Sage.

鼎

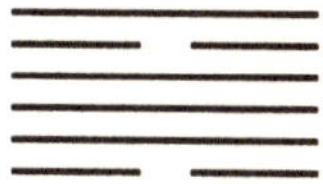

50. TING/THE CALDRON

You serve as an example to others by sacrificing your ego and accepting the guidance of the Higher Power.

The hexagram Ting concerns the nourishment and guidance one must have in order to fully succeed. While the culture around us often encourages us to "take charge" and make aggressive demands on life, the *I Ching* offers far wiser counsel. Here we are encouraged to give up the incessant demands of our ego—to deepen our humility and acceptance and to listen carefully to the instructions of the Sage.

The image of the caldron concerns your inner thoughts: whatever you hold in the "caldron" of your mind is your offering to the Higher Power. The quality of assistance you can receive from the universe is governed by the quality of your offering. If you constantly indulge in the concerns of the ego—fears, desires, strategies to control, harshness toward others—you repel the Higher Power and block your own nourishment. If, on the other hand, you consciously let go of your resistance to life and hold quiet and correct thoughts, you become receptive to the Creative and your continual nourishment is assured.

Ting comes to suggest that the wisest thing that you can do now is to still your ego and conscientiously enter into a conversation with the Sage. To influence others, or to achieve a proper goal, follow the same path. By cultivating humility and acceptance, purifying your inner thoughts, and concentrating on that which is good and innocent and true, you summon the power of the Creative and meet with good fortune in the outer world.

FIRST LINE Turn the caldron of your self upside down and pour out what is inferior. By purifying yourself of bad habits and attitudes now you make possible outstanding achievements.

SECOND LINE Others may envy and seek to test the superior person. Concentrate on remaining innocent and correct, and you will not be harmed.

THIRD LINE The superior person is always recognized in due time. If you do not have the influence you would like, consider whether you may be blocked by some assertion of your ego.

FOURTH LINE A position of influence is a position of responsibility. Neglecting your character now invites a humiliation.

FIFTH LINE One who remains modest and open, and who retreats from what is inferior whenever it appears, will have help in times of difficulty.

SIXTH LINE Counsel others as the Sage counsels you: through making an example of correctness, through quiet perseverance, and through gentleness.

震

THUNDER

THUNDER

51. CHÊN/THE AROUSING (SHOCK)

The shock of unsettling events
brings fear and trembling.
Move toward a higher
truth and all will
be well.

The tendency of human beings is to rely on the strategies of the ego: desiring, plotting, and striving. When we exercise the ego, our spiritual development stops, and the universe must use shocking events to move us back onto the path. The appearance of the hexagram Chên indicates an immediate need for self-examination, self-correction, and a redevotion to following the path of the Sage.

In Chinese, the hexagram translates to mean "thunder over thunder": a continuing series of shocks occurs until the obstruction in our attitude is removed. It is important not to react against these shocks. Instead, quiet and open your mind, accept that what is happening has come to teach you a specific and necessary lesson, and look inside to see where you are resisting the will of the Higher Power. The sooner you return to innocence and acceptance, the sooner the shocks will subside.

Those who maintain a reverence for proper principles and an inner commitment to higher things are unperturbed by shocking events; they simply concentrate on deepening their understanding. If you find yourself feeling threatened by circumstances, withdraw into stillness and meditation. The only remedy for doubt and fear is a reconnection with higher truth.

Shock is an important and beneficial teacher to those who follow the path of the Sage. Make good use of this new beginning and good fortune results.

FIRST LINE Shock frightens us and at first we are convinced that it is bad. When we learn the lesson it has come to teach, we are thankful for it.

SECOND LINE Do not resist unpleasant circumstances. If you withdraw into contemplation you can regain what has been lost.

THIRD LINE Do not let the shock of fate propel you into negative conduct. Steadfastly resist the temptation of the inferiors, open your mind, and a way through will be shown.

FOURTH LINE You are mired in resistance to events. Quiet your ego, accept the situation, and open your heart to learning what you need to learn.

FIFTH LINE Repeated shocks occur. Quietness and truth are the best refuge. One who stays centered is unmoved and unharmed.

SIXTH LINE Engagement with shocking events robs you of peace of mind, inviting disaster. Withdrawal into stillness restores your balance and prevents misfortune.

艮

MOUNTAIN

MOUNTAIN

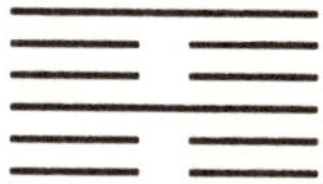

52. KÊN/ KEEPING STILL, MOUNTAIN

Still your emotions through meditation.

Receiving this hexagram is a sign that you need to quiet your emotions so that you can think clearly. To answer the clamorings of the ego with action now is to invite misfortune. The *I Ching* counsels nonaction and the stilling of the emotions through meditation.

It is in the nature of having a body to have strong feelings and impulses. However, if we allow our thinking to be controlled by them, we cannot act with the gentleness, neutrality, and graceful wisdom of the Sage. Instead, we move rashly when we ought to keep still, or we solidify when we ought to remain fluid. Therefore it is necessary to quiet the body and its inferior elements so that our thoughts and actions may be clear and balanced.

Three things are advised. First, sit quietly in a self-supporting position with your back straight and eyes closed. Second, observe the flow of your bodily emotions. Do not judge or resist them; the simple practice of watching them come, linger, and go without acting on them allows you to gradually separate them from your thought processes. Third, turn your inner conflicts over to the Deity for resolution.

The help of the Higher Power is only made available to those who ask for it in a disciplined way, who make an offering of their stillness and mindfulness. Through meditation we reduce the influence of the inferior elements and make it possible for the Sage to assist us. Keep still as a mountain now and you will be rewarded with good fortune.

FIRST LINE It is not a time to move. It is easier to still yourself now than after action has been initiated. Remain innocent, quiet, and detached.

SECOND LINE There is a great desire to move, but the time is not right. Let others do what they will, and hold to stillness and acceptance. This enables the Sage to do his work.

THIRD LINE Do not attempt to force a good feeling into place. Patiently let go of doubt, fear, anger, and distrust. The Sage aids those who quietly accept the Unknown.

FOURTH LINE A heart at rest leads to a mind at rest. Deepening your acceptance leads to good fortune.

FIFTH LINE Restrain your speech. An active tongue betrays a restless mind. Tranquility on every level is advised.

SIXTH LINE Perseverance in stillness, in both thought and deed, forms a noble heart. The ultimate fruit of a noble heart is complete peace of mind.

漸

WIND

MOUNTAIN

53. CHIEN/ DEVELOPMENT (GRADUAL PROGRESS)

Those who persevere make continuous progress.

The image of this hexagram is that of a tree growing high on a mountaintop. If this tree grows too fast, without first properly rooting itself, it becomes susceptible to being torn up and destroyed by the winds. If, however, it establishes a proper foundation and is content to grow gradually, it will enjoy a long life and a lofty view.

Human beings are no different. While we often desire rapid progress—we want to change someone's mind *today*, obtain an apology *now*, achieve all our goals *immediately*—sooner or later we must come to understand that the only lasting progress is gradual progress. Chien comes to urge you to accept that fact and base your thoughts, attitudes, and actions upon it.

When we have allowed ourselves to be pulled off balance by another or by some event, the ego tempts us to believe that we can influence the situation through forceful behavior. This is incorrect; the actions of the ego inevitably complicate our difficulties. The greatest influence possible always comes through the patient and steady refinement of one's inner self. If you will devote yourself to the path of the Sage, with every step along that path you will be strengthened, and progress will come automatically. It will be gradual, but it will last.

Be patient, modest, and accepting now. Life often demands that we wait longer than we might like for some change, and the only true comfort available during these times is the knowledge that we are steadfastly developing ourselves into superior people. In time, every honor comes to those who are persevering and correct.

FIRST LINE The early stages of self-development are often tinged with anxiety and doubt. Do not be swayed by these inferior influences. Persevere in what is correct and progress will be made.

SECOND LINE A beneficial development can cause us to become selfish and careless. Share the good with others and remain conscientious.

THIRD LINE Do not enter rashly into a conflict. Stand quietly in the center and keep your balance. This enables a true and lasting resolution to be found.

FOURTH LINE Nonresistance is the wisest course at this time. By willingly yielding to events you save yourself for a more beneficial hour.

FIFTH LINE As you develop yourself you will inevitably be misunderstood by others. Endure these times patiently, and they will pass. By staying on the path unswervingly you meet with great success.

SIXTH LINE When we hold strictly to what is correct, the Creative is happy to help us in all things. One who follows this course gains the world and serves as an inspiring example to his fellow men.

歸妹

THUNDER

LAKE

54. KUEI MEI/THE MARRYING MAIDEN

In relationships, desires lead to misfortune.
Behave with discipline and balance.

Kuei Mei is concerned with the guidelines for the proper conduct of relationships, whether they be social, romantic, or work related. The image here is of thunder roiling the surface of a lake, and it suggests that relationships can be disturbing to our peace of mind unless they are established and governed under proper principles.

The nature of relationships is that they lead us into the desire state: we begin to desire another, desire recognition, desire retribution, desire a particular outcome in a given situation. All of these desires lead us away from the equanimity that we aim to maintain as students of the *I Ching*. This hexagram often comes as a sign that you are in danger of sacrificing your composure in an effort to affect a relationship.

When someone does not treat you as you would like, you are faced with a choice as to what to do. While it may be tempting to abandon the relationship in anger or act aggressively to produce a result, neither of these is consistent with proper principles. You are counseled instead to return to inner independence, acceptance, modesty, and gentleness. The greatest influence is always had through inner discipline and balance; less subtle measures may produce more immediate results, but they are seldom lasting.

This hexagram also teaches us that rushing into a relationship, rushing to resolve a relationship, or rushing to escape a relationship are all akin to rushing on ice: each invites a painful fall. Seek to establish relationships slowly and on proper principles, to allow them to evolve naturally, and to resolve disputes with patience and reserve. If your primary relationship—that with the Sage—is open and ongoing and devoted, then all other relationships will fall into place.

FIRST LINE The possibility of having an influence is small. Do not react against the adversity, but retreat into stillness and patience. Good fortune comes to one who accepts a background position.

SECOND LINE Though outer conditions appear unpromising, a success is possible if you look faithfully for the good in others, yourself, and the situation.

THIRD LINE The ego encourages improper desires and self-indulgences. Do not tempt fate by adopting a lax attitude.

FOURTH LINE A good result comes in its own time. Do not waste yourself in trying to hurry it. The greatest gifts come to those who remain composed and patient.

FIFTH LINE Disdain for those below or envy of those above prevents your progress. Strive not to achieve a goal or to have an influence but to embody proper virtues. In this way your success is assured.

SIXTH LINE Correct conduct is empty unless our hearts are also devoted. Success is only possible when we abandon our own agendas and follow the way of the Sage.

豐

THUNDER

FIRE

55. FÊNG/ ABUNDANCE (FULLNESS)

A moment of great influence is at hand.
Prepare wisely and act accordingly.

The image of the hexagram Fêng is that of thunder and lightning filling the sky. It signifies a period of tremendous power which, like all such moments, only lasts for a time. Here we are instructed how to know when the moment is ripe, and what to do when it is not.

Our influence in the world naturally ebbs and flows. At one moment others are full of mistrust, and forward movement is impossible. In the next, by steadfastly clinging to what is true and good, we reawaken their receptivity and growth can take place. Only by carefully observing these cycles—the openings and closings of others to our influence—can we achieve greatness. To do this, we must cultivate an attitude of independent watchfulness. In this state of quiet observation we open our hearts to the aid of the Sage, who in turn opens our eyes to what is possible and what is not. This clarity enables us to move with strength and grace when the time is right, and in this we achieve abundance.

Fêng also advises us that influence cannot last forever; as the sun rises, so must it set. When receptivity gives way to mistrust and our influence begins to wane, we ought not struggle to fortify or prolong it. Modesty and detachment require that we accept the turning of the tide. By letting go of the passing moment and entering the next with a correct and balanced attitude, we save ourselves for a more beneficial time.

FIRST LINE The potential for an influential union exists. Maintain clarity and balance and act energetically when the way opens. When it closes, withdraw without resistance.

SECOND LINE Mistrust and envy make having an influence impossible. Inferior elements will disperse if you hold firmly to inner truth.

THIRD LINE Egos soar and the opportunity for influence is eclipsed. Let go of anything that is incorrect and wait patiently. The Higher Power will come to your aid if you do this now.

FOURTH LINE The darkness gives way if you relate properly. Energy joined to modesty brings good fortune.

FIFTH LINE When we cling to truth and humility, what is needed comes without delay. The path of the Sage is constantly showered with blessings, and so are you if you stay upon it.

SIXTH LINE If you make improper use of abundance, misfortune results. Pride and harshness toward others fell your own roof and leave you in the rain.

旅

FIRE
MOUNTAIN

56. LÜ/THE WANDERER

We are all wanderers in the Unknown.
Those who travel beside the Sage
are protected from harm.

A person who travels as a stranger in a strange land is wise to display an attitude free of arrogance and belligerence. Otherwise he is liable to meet with trouble and find himself unable to survive it. With this hexagram the *I Ching* reminds us that we are all strangers in a strange land, wanderers in a vast and unknowable universe, obliged to act accordingly.

Think of how you would proceed if traveling alone in an unfamiliar country. You would be cautious and reserved, taking great care not to fall in with the wrong people or enter into dangerous places. You would be tolerant of others and generous toward them if a dispute arose, and you would be inclined to settle disagreements quickly to keep them from getting out of hand. You would rely on your attentiveness, your modest attitude, and your gentle manner to keep you out of harm's way. The hexagram Lü comes to remind you that it is wise to travel through your entire life in this fashion.

Seek now to stay in quiet harmony with the Higher Power and to embody caution, modesty, and generosity in your actions. Do not drag out disagreements with others; conflict is a prison that grows more dangerous every minute you are in it. Do not depart from the path of humility and correct conduct; in doing so, you lose the protection of the Deity and risk misfortune. By continually seeking to serve the innocent and the good, you stay in step with the Sage and never wander alone in the world.

FIRST LINE The wanderer should not involve himself with inferior things. Cling to the essential and the correct in your thoughts and actions.

SECOND LINE The wanderer who is modest and generous in spirit always has a resting place and the allegiance of steadfast friends.

THIRD LINE The wanderer who is meddlesome and egotistical quickly loses his resting place. The current situation becomes dangerous if you do not return to neutrality and detachment.

FOURTH LINE Desire and mistrust keep you from finding ease. Peace of mind comes when we let go of ambitions and fears and follow the Sage from moment to moment.

FIFTH LINE Through inner and outer correctness we assure our own good fortune. What is entered into with humility and generosity meets with success.

SIXTH LINE One must not abandon the inner attitude of the wanderer. Through carelessness you can quickly lose all that you have gained.

巽

WIND
WIND

57. SUN/THE GENTLE (THE PENETRATING, WIND)

Consistent correctness turns every situation to your advantage.

The image of this hexagram is that of a gentle wind dispersing storm clouds. A wind that changes direction often, even a very powerful one, will disperse nothing—it only stirs up the sky. The wind that causes real change is the one that blows consistently in the same direction. There is an important lesson for us in this example.

When faced with a difficult problem to resolve or a goal we wish to achieve, we often are tempted to take striking and energetic actions. Though it is possible to achieve temporary results in this fashion, they tend to collapse when we cannot sustain the vigorous effort. More enduring accomplishments are won through gentle but ceaseless penetration, like that of a soft wind blowing steadily in the same direction. The truth of the Sage penetrates to us in this way, and this hexagram comes now to remind you that this is how you should seek to penetrate to others.

The advice given to you by the *I Ching* is threefold. First, establish a clear goal; the wind that continually changes direction has no real effect. Second, apply the principle of gentle penetration to yourself; by eliminating your own inferior qualities you earn an influence over others. Third, avoid aggressive or ambitious maneuvers now; these are rooted in desire and fear and will only serve to block the aid of the Creative. The desirable influence is the one that flows naturally from maintaining a proper attitude.

In your interactions with others, bend like the willow. By remaining adaptable, balanced, accepting, and independent, and by steadily moving in a single direction, you gain the clarity and strength that make possible a series of great successes.

FIRST LINE You must be as resolute as a warrior against doubt and mistrust. When you can advance in correctness, do so. When you cannot, retreat without hesitation.

SECOND LINE A hidden enemy threatens. Search your subconscious for negative influences. The aid of a counselor can be beneficial in this.

THIRD LINE When your insight penetrates to the source of the problem, do not dwell on it. The ego will become entangled. Simply make the necessary correction, and persevere in it.

FOURTH LINE When we are resolutely modest, independent, and correct, our external difficulties magically pass away and success is assured.

FIFTH LINE The beginning has not been good, but progress is still possible. Carefully disengage from bad habits, and remain steadfast in following proper principles. Things change for the better.

SIXTH LINE Sometimes the inferior enemy cannot be identified. Do not struggle, but quietly return to improving yourself. In this way a good result can still be obtained.

兑

LAKE

LAKE

58. TUI/THE JOYOUS, LAKE

True joy is experienced by those
who are strong within and gentle without.

The hexagram Tui teaches us how to come into possession of joy. In our search for success and happiness we are prone to think that we must take aggressive actions to achieve them. The instruction of the *I Ching* is just the opposite: only those who practice innocence, acceptance, and detachment inherit true joy in this world.

We often see around us how forcible effort brings about what appears to be progress. Our egos tempt us to believe that these gains are lasting and valuable, but the truth is otherwise. Whatever is won by the desirous, ambitious, demanding manipulations of the ego will soon be lost. Others can always be temporarily browbeaten into doing things our way, but only hearts won by friendliness and sincere goodwill are true over time.

The *I Ching* teaches us again and again that joy and success cannot be forced or stolen. They are achieved gradually—but steadily—by those who relate correctly to others and to the Higher Power. To relate correctly means to steadfastly practice innocence, detachment, acceptance, modesty, and gentleness. Life is full of shortcuts, but this is the only route that leads to true joy.

The image of the hexagram is that of two lakes joined together to keep from drying up. It is an encouragement to us to join with like-minded friends now in the discussion and contemplation of higher things. If we engage in an ongoing conversation about proper principles with our friends, our relationship to truth is steady and our ego cannot seduce us into the doubt, fear, and anxiety that lead away from joy.

In your heart, be firm in holding to what is good and honest and correct. In your thoughts and actions, be gentle and accepting. Those who persevere on this path will meet with true joy and lasting success.

FIRST LINE In detachment there is freedom and contentment. One who empties himself of all desire now finds himself awash with joy.

SECOND LINE Those who are sincere in resisting inferior influences meet with good fortune. Those who abandon correctness for temporary pleasures do not.

THIRD LINE If we are not firm within, there will be trouble without. Be on guard against envy, ambition, and desires. Joy is the province of the innocent and the independent.

FOURTH LINE If you sacrifice principles for a momentary pleasure or gain, you will never know true joy. Inner conflict ends when we turn our hearts and minds permanently to what is higher.

FIFTH LINE One who dabbles in inferior emotions, attitudes, and actions will be undone by them. Let these things go and return to innocence and truth.

SIXTH LINE If we become caught up in the cares of the world, sooner or later we will be destroyed. Detachment, humility, and acceptance save us from this fate.

渙

59. HUAN/DISPERSION (DISSOLUTION)

Disperse hard attitudes with gentleness.

The hexagram Huan comes to indicate that there are rigidity and harshness present, either in yourself or others, and that they should be dissolved now for the benefit of all. Whenever we fall into a negative state such as judgment, anger, fear, anxiety, or desire, our attitude becomes structured and inflexible. As long as we remain in this condition we cannot receive the assistance of the Higher Power. Therefore, if we wish for a return of good fortune now we must take steps to dissolve the hardness.

The image of Huan is that of a warm spring wind steadily dissolving winter ice. This is meant to teach us that it is through perseverance and gentleness—rather than aggressiveness—that we overcome what is hard. The *I Ching* counsels the use of religious forces now: employ music, prayer, meditation, a common project, or some other form of sacred concentration or ceremony to release the pent-up energy in yourself and others.

Allow harsh and unforgiving feelings to be carried away by the song of a flute, the reverberation of a drum, or the sound of the wind through the trees. In your mind's eye, see where the flow of positive energy is blocked, and then imagine this place as an ice floe breaking up in a thawing river.

Until the inflexibility is removed there can be no unity, either within your own spirit, with others, or with the Sage. Remember that inferior emotions are hard, where the attitudes of the superior person—acceptance, detachment, modesty, innocence, and equanimity—have a quality of softness to them. By returning to this now you insure your own good fortune.

FIRST LINE Misunderstandings should be healed as early as possible. Take action to restore trust and good faith now.

SECOND LINE A moderate view of others' transgressions is always best. In patience and gentleness we discover the source of their obstructions and also our own.

THIRD LINE You will have to dissolve your grievances and desires and unstructure your attitude if you are to succeed now.

FOURTH LINE Sometimes it is necessary to sacrifice an attitude, a relationship, or a short-term goal in order to stay on the path of correctness. The superior person does this willingly and meets with good fortune.

FIFTH LINE By gathering yourself and others around a great ideal you disperse negative influences. The superior person uses this method to heal misunderstandings.

SIXTH LINE If you focus on negative feelings you create a dangerous situation. Lead yourself and others away from misfortune by adhering to modesty, neutrality, and calm acceptance.

節

WATER

LAKE

60. CHIEH/LIMITATION

Voluntarily chosen limits empower your growth.

The practice of economies is a valuable notion everywhere in life. In your financial dealings, a reasonable thrift practiced today assures you of opportunity tomorrow. In your emotional life, the practice of balance and equanimity allows steady spiritual progress. The hexagram Chieh comes as an encouragement to set practical limits throughout your life.

Life lived without guidelines is confusing and troubling. In order to make genuine progress in any direction, we must first give some definition to our path. However, limits that are overstrenuous are not helpful; having too many rules causes rebellion in the one on whom they are imposed, whether one's self or another. Therefore there must be limits even on one's limits.

To yourself, the setting of limits means defining your purpose and responsibilities so that you have a clear idea of where your energies are to be aimed. Your limits should be determined by yourself, not another or the culture in which you live. Avoid harshness and impatience with yourself; true progress is made in gradual steps. Allow yourself pleasure, but avoid careless self-indulgence.

With others, place limits both on your own actions and the indulgences you offer them. To encourage another's inferior qualities is to invite misfortune. Allow your interactions with others to take place within the limits of gentleness, tolerance, and innocence. If you will define and observe reasonable limits in all things, you will be assured of steady progress.

FIRST LINE A desired development is still constrained. Recognize the limitation and avoid forceful action. Help comes to a disciplined person.

SECOND LINE When obstacles dissolve, seize the day. Anxious hesitation causes stagnation.

THIRD LINE Do not engage in egotistical extravagances. Follow the truth without other ambitions. Correct your mistakes as you become aware of them.

FOURTH LINE Accept natural limitations. Where there is an opening, go forward with balance. When the way is closed, withdraw willingly into stillness.

FIFTH LINE Any limitation you would impose on another must first be accepted and practiced by yourself. Be gentle, innocent, and truthful in all things now.

SIXTH LINE Avoid severity with others at all costs. Be gentle with yourself unless a strong hand is necessary to insure your correctness. Move toward truth without swerving.

中孚

WIND
LAKE

61. CHUNG FU/ INNER TRUTH

Through openness and gentleness
the correct solution is reached.

Arriving at the correct solution to a difficult situation requires a receptivity to inner truth. Unless we are willing to put aside the strong emotions of our egos and devote ourselves to discovering what is right, there can be no hope of progress at this time. Help only comes when we invite it with a sincere and innocent attitude.

The *I Ching* teaches a simple but effective method of influencing difficult people and arduous situations. It advises us first to lay aside our prejudices—our feelings of being wounded, angry, or in the right—and second to seek to understand the positions of others and the lesson that the Sage is teaching us with the situation. Even when another is truly out of line, it is only by accepting this and remaining balanced that you make it possible for positive change to occur. Gentleness and understanding create in others an unconscious willingness to be led.

The superior person therefore avoids the use of anger and force in trying times, knowing that they only prolong conflict. It is far wiser to accept that each experience we have is necessary for us to learn something about ourselves and about the higher laws of life. The greatest openings come when we meet difficulty with acceptance, gentleness, and a desire to understand the lesson underneath.

FIRST LINE Strength belongs to those who are inwardly and outwardly devoted to what is good. Examine yourself for negative habits and let go of them before they cause a fall.

SECOND LINE Inner strength or weakness is always being communicated to others. If you are devoted to higher things, that will be felt. If you are not, that too will be felt.

THIRD LINE If you rely on another for your peace of mind, your balance is lost. Be neither flattered nor dismayed at fluctuations in another's affections. By maintaining inner independence you successfully negotiate the path.

FOURTH LINE One must recognize the source of one's power in order to maintain it. When your ego takes credit for progress, misfortune follows. When you acknowledge the help of the Sage, good fortune continues.

FIFTH LINE Your quiet strength and devotion to inner truth can create unity where now there is chaos. Correct yourself meticulously and others will follow you.

SIXTH LINE Do not try to talk others into accepting truth. Self-development is made step by step, and each must find his own pace. Reticence toward others and innocence in your own attitude is advised.

小過

THUNDER

MOUNTAIN

62. HSIAO KUO/ PREPONDERANCE OF THE SMALL

In a great storm the wise bird returns
to her nest and waits patiently.

This is a time of difficult and dangerous conditions. You should not be seduced into struggling, striving, or seeking solutions through aggressive action. Success is met only by waiting modestly for the guidance of the Creative.

Trying times are a test of our integrity and commitment to proper principles. The ordinary person reacts to challenges with fear, anger, mistrust of fate, and a stubborn desire to strike out and eliminate difficulty once and for all. While the temptation to act in this way can be great, to do so can only lead to misfortune and the loss of hard-won ground.

The way of the superior person faced with difficulty is that of nonaction rather than action. She does not strive after recognition or resolution or attempt to gain a higher position by conquering others. Instead, she retreats into her center and cultivates humility, patience, and conscientiousness. On the path of acceptance, self-inquiry, and self-improvement we obtain the aid of the Creative and meet with success after the storm has passed.

FIRST LINE Trying to fly before it is time causes one to fall. Hold to nonaction and allow the Creative to do its work.

SECOND LINE The situation is not ready to be resolved. The way is shown to one who waits modestly and patiently.

THIRD LINE The time calls for great care. Do not relax into egotistical behaviors. Persevere in what is correct or misfortune results.

FOURTH LINE The temptation to act harshly wells up. Do not give in to your inferiors. By yielding the matter to the Sage you meet with good fortune.

FIFTH LINE One cannot succeed without the aid of others. Seek company and the counsel of those who are sincerely devoted to Higher Truth.

SIXTH LINE Pressing on forcefully and immodestly invites disaster. Return to the path of humility and devotion to proper principles, and a great misfortune will be avoided.

既濟

WATER

FIRE

63. CHI CHI/AFTER COMPLETION

Good fortune unfolds for those who remain on guard against inferior influences.

This hexagram indicates that the movement from chaos to order is complete. The time is extremely favorable and you are likely to enjoy much success as long as you heed the warning of Chi Chi: remain on guard against incorrect thoughts, attitudes, and actions, both in yourself and in others.

We arrive in beneficial situations by following the path of correct conduct. When we have achieved success or are close to it, it is in our nature to want to relax and allow the ego to bask in glory. If you revert to this sort of carelessness now you will undo all that you have worked to build. It is important not to become indifferent to spiritual details at this time: if a thought or action even borders on incorrectness, discard it and return to the path of the Sage immediately. One minute we dip our toe in incorrectness, the next minute we are swimming in it, and the next we drown. Therefore it is wiser to simply keep our toes dry in the first place.

You are also counseled to remain alert to inferior influences in others. You can only prevent misfortunes by anticipating them in advance, and this is achieved through watchfulness.

The image of Chi Chi is that of a kettle of water boiling over a fire. There is great power here, but it is lost if one allows the water to boil over or evaporate through carelessness and indifference. Alertness and conscientious adherence to what is correct are called for if you wish to prolong your good fortune now.

FIRST LINE To get drunk on the possibility of success and rush carelessly forward invites a disaster. Proceed slowly and thoughtfully and your progress will endure.

SECOND LINE If you do not have the cooperation or recognition of others, do not chase after it or condemn them harshly. Through modesty and acceptance you gain your objectives.

THIRD LINE You lose what you have gained if you allow your inferior qualities to take over. Chaos is avoided through conscientious correctness.

FOURTH LINE The best of times quickly turn sour if we relax into carelessness. Be on guard at all times.

FIFTH LINE The Higher Power looks not only at our actions but into our hearts to gauge our worthiness. Through genuine inner modesty, acceptance, and innocence you correct your own errors and set an example for others.

SIXTH LINE If you stop to admire your grace in crossing the stream you will slip and fall. By steadfastly keeping your eye on what is correct you insure your good fortune.

未濟

FIRE
WATER

64. WEI CHI/ BEFORE COMPLETION

The transition from chaos to order depends upon your achieving true inner calm.

The image of this hexagram is that of spring, a time when the darkness and decay of winter are about to give way to the light and plenty of summer. The transition is not yet complete; here it depends upon you strengthening your clarity, calm, and conscientiousness.

Wei Chi often comes as an indication that we have not yet achieved a genuine inner equanimity. As long as we respond to outer pressures with our egos—by worrying, desiring, or becoming aggressive—we cannot attain a successful repose. The *I Ching* reminds us now to abandon the hysterics of the ego in favor of acceptance, modesty, and inner balance.

Wei Chi denotes a time of great responsibility. In a very real sense it can be said that the state of the world depends upon *your* thoughts and conduct now. The external world will only come into order if the inner world has done so. Therefore, seek now to correct whatever in your self is at odds with the principles of the Sage. Quiet your ego, make humility and acceptance your primary goals, and move forward like a fox walking on ice: cautiously, deliberately, and gently. By persevering in what is true and good you build the foundation upon which good fortune can come to rest.

FIRST LINE There is a temptation to try to make rapid progress. An unbalanced enthusiasm only leads to failure and humiliation. Innocent nonaction is advised at this time.

SECOND LINE It is a time to wait, but you must not lose sight of the goal. To rescue yourself and others, stay tuned to inner truth. Do not indulge in egotistical fantasies now.

THIRD LINE A transition is possible, but one must be correct in every measure. Only by filling yourself with gentleness, goodness, and devotion to truth can you succeed.

FOURTH LINE In times of struggle, perseverance on the path is everything. To waver from what is correct in thought or action is to risk losing all that you have gained.

FIFTH LINE The superior person is steadfast in the ways of the Sage and thus meets with unqualified success.

SIXTH LINE Do not exercise your ego when things change for the better. By remaining disciplined and modest you insure continued good fortune.

KEY FOR IDENTIFYING THE HEXAGRAMS

TRIGRAMS								
UPPER ▶ / LOWER ▼	CH'IEN ☰ *Heaven*	CHÊN ☳ *Thunder*	K'AN ☵ *Water*	KÊN ☶ *Mountain*	K'UN ☷ *Earth*	SUN ☴ *Wind*	LI ☲ *Fire*	TUI ☱ *Lake*
CH'IEN ☰ *Heaven*	1	34	5	26	11	9	14	43
CHÊN ☳ *Thunder*	25	51	3	27	24	42	21	17
K'AN ☵ *Water*	6	40	29	4	7	59	64	47
KÊN ☶ *Mountain*	33	62	39	52	15	53	56	31
K'UN ☷ *Earth*	12	16	8	23	2	20	35	45
SUN ☴ *Wind*	44	32	48	18	46	57	50	28
LI ☲ *Fire*	13	55	63	22	36	37	30	49
TUI ☱ *Lake*	10	54	60	41	19	61	38	58